Why, God?

Suffering Through Cancer into Faith

MARGARET CARLISLE CUPIT
with her grandfather
EDWARD HUGH HENDERSON

Foreword by David Hein

RESOURCE *Publications* · Eugene, Oregon

WHY, GOD?
Suffering Through Cancer into Faith

Resource Publications
An Imprint of Wipf and Stock Publishers
199 W. 8th Ave., Suite 3
Eugene, OR 97401

www.wipfandstock.com

ISBN 13: 978-1-62564-478-7

Manufactured in the U.S.A.   01/29/2015

To St. Jude Children's Research Hospital
and all those who bring hope to the fight against childhood cancer

Sooner or later life is going to lead you (as it did Jesus) into the belly of the beast, into a place where you can't fix it, you can't control it, and you can't explain it or understand it. That's where transformation most easily happens. That's when you're uniquely in the hands of God.[1]

—Richard Rohr

We must put our confidence in truth. But that doesn't mean sitting back and waiting for the truth to shine from above ... It means following with devoted obedience the truth we have seen as true, with an entire confidence in God, that he will correct, clear, and redirect our vision, to the perception of a freer and deeper truth. Go with the truth you have and let it carry you into collision with the hard rocks of fact, and then you'll learn something.[2]

—Austin Farrer

1. Rohr, "Suffering Can Bring Us to God," para. 3.
2. Farrer, *End of Man*, 104.

Contents

List of Photographs | ix
Foreword by David Hein | xi
Acknowledgments | xv
Introduction | xxi

1 The Hard Rocks of Reality | 1

2 But I Have Plans | 6

3 This Place is St. Jude | 17

4 Of Squirrels and Theology | 33

5 Why, God? | 46

6 Sacramental Experiences | 71

7 The Hidden Kingdom | 81

8 Choosing Life, Staying the Course | 109

9 Something I Can't See | 135

10 Epilogue: Embracing Darkness, Seeing Light | 140

Bibliography | 145
Suggested Theological Reading | 146

Photographs

Figure 1: Before treatment: Maggie with her mother Ellie: May, 2010 | 101

Figure 2: Treatments begin: June, 2010 | 102

Figure 3: Confidence before surgery: summer, 2010 | 102

Figure 4: Maggie with NP Patti Peas and Dr. Alberto Pappo: summer, 2010 | 103

Figure 5: Battling cancer with Baby Kya: late summer, 2010 | 103

Figure 6: Halloween at St. Jude: NP Patti Peas, Maggie, Dr. Beth Stewart | 104

Figure 7: Visitors from Baton Rouge: Grandpapa, Maggie, Nini, Flynn: autumn, 2010 | 104

Figure 8: Best Christmas ever: Anne Houston (Sissy), Maggie, Flynn, grandmother Anne | 105

Figure 9: A terrible treatment after Christmas: January, 2011 | 105

Figure 10: Odie Comforts Maggie | 106

Figure 11: Maggie, Carissa, Odie, Flynn, and Rachel before the Prom: April, 2011 | 106

Figure 12: Annual St. Jude Marathon, December, 2011: Anne, Anne Houston, Flynn, Maggie, Ellie, Paul | 107

Figure 13: Rhodes College Graduation: Anne Houston, Ellie, Anne, Maggie, Flynn: May, 2014 | 107

Figure 14: Celebrating Graduation with her St. Jude Team: NP Patti Peas, Dr. Alberto Pappo, chaplain Lisa Anderson, NP Valerie Pappo, Maggie, Dr. Beth Stewart, Dr. Liza Johnson, RN Julie Morganelli: May, 2014 | 108

Foreword

In the 2003 movie *Open Range*, a western starring Kevin Costner and Robert Duvall, the latter's character, Boss Spearman, is standing at a freshly dug grave with his partner, Charley Waite, played by Costner. Before Waite extemporizes some prayerful sentences for a murdered colleague, he asks Spearman if he'd like to say a few words. No, Boss replies, "I'll be holdin' a grudge" against the Man Upstairs, "that Son of a Bitch," for letting a good man die a violent death. Charley Waite understands. Later we learn that Boss Spearman's wife and daughter are dead—killed not by outlaws or by hostiles, but by typhus.

Few theists would admit this fact in public, but undoubtedly many of them who suffer calamitous loss for no good reason hold thoughts not unlike Spearman's and might employ similar contemptuous phrases when contemplating the Lord and his mysterious ways and wondrous works. How could relatively innocent people suffer so horrendously when truly horrible men and women get off comparatively scot-free?

Most religious people today, notwithstanding their overt party labels, are probably Deists, telling pollsters they believe in God but consciously drawing no connections between divine causation and current events.

Or, like the ancients, contemporary Westerners are worshipers of *Moira* (Fate) or believers in *Tyche* (Chance). The former might sagely observe that *Everything happens for a reason*, a reason buried in the logic of an inscrutable Force. Of course, not knowing whether this Ultimate Cause is life-giving or death-dealing somewhat undermines the efficacy of this bromide in everyday life. And among the latter—the worldly worshipers of Lady Luck—can be found a modern woman who offers her forty-five-year-old best friend, recently diagnosed with malignant myeloma and given three years—outside—to live, the wisdom of the Wheel of Fortune.

Then there are the sentimentalists, for whom a little theology is a dangerous thing: "Jesus took my two-year-old girl to be with him in heaven 'cause she was just too good for this world." And when the unsentimental reader scans these words in the obits of his daily newspaper, he shakes his head and mutters, *Yes: what a friend we have in Jesus*; and he feels confirmed in his decision not to return to church after college.

The form of evil hardest to take is the type that appears in events such as earthquakes and tsunamis and in diseases like typhus and cancer, particularly when the victims are young people. Of the two forms of evil, moral evil can be attributed to man's perverted will; but natural evil, including disease, is not so easily comprehended within a moral reckoning of God and neighbor.

Every now and then some people will still trace a horrific affliction back to the sins of the individual or his fathers, as in the case of the Elephant Man. But since the book of Job, independent-minded monotheists have questioned the likelihood of this interpretation, and since the story of Jesus and the man born blind (John 9:1–3), no Christian has been authorized to blame diseases on innocent victims. But if not that justification—grounded in a rational, if obscure, moral calculus—then what is the source of or reason for suffering and evil in a world created and sustained and indeed governed by a God historically understood to be nothing less than Love Almighty?

Philosophers have made many attempts to justify the ways of God to man, and their theories, such as the Augustinian free-will defense and the Irenaean view of this world as a vale of soul-making, are well known. In recent years, however, theologians have understood that these explanations may be unhelpful to actual, not merely theoretical, sufferers. Hence they have learned what many Christians already knew: to do theodicy practically.

Practical theodicy is concerned to discover the causes of suffering and to try to remove them; to talk less and listen more; to perceive Christ suffering alongside the victim. Jesus is seen as one who does not rationalize the mystery of God's universe but stands—or sits or lies or kneels—alongside the afflicted as the divine-human fellow-sufferer who understands (Whitehead) or as the one who offers a life in which to live rather than an explanation that leaves a person just as dead—psychologically or spiritually or physically—as she was before (Farrer).

These two approaches to theodicy—theoretical and practical—may be roped together. This result is the aim of a practical philosophical theology: bringing the insights of philosophical theology into the lives of ordinary sufferers, who, as intelligent beings, often need not just a shoulder to lean on, or trite palliative phrases, but honest, thought-provoking, caring wisdom in words that invite but never dictate.

Which brings us to this book, a dual inquiry that focuses on the physical, intellectual, and spiritual struggles of Maggie Cupit. A young woman who had expected to spend a recent summer as a research intern at the St. Jude Children's Research Hospital, Maggie instead finds herself there as a patient being treated for a life-threatening bone cancer. A highly intelligent and deeply compassionate student at Rhodes College in Memphis, Tennessee, she is not a simple believer in mere Christianity: pat answers and glib explanations will not suffice for this thoroughly modern Maggie. As she confronts serious intellectual questions posed by her cancer and others' illnesses, she also searches for a way to inhabit a world she loves but which has shown itself to be harsh and apparently indifferent.

Why, God? Suffering Through Cancer into Faith is an account of Maggie's growth into faith through a journey that includes suffering, uncertainty about life and death, a web of supportive relationships, the loss of friends she'd become close to, and an encounter with an understanding of God that she could not accept. *Open Range*'s Boss Spearman and Maggie would have understood one another. But, in the midst of her own real-world drama, a better conversation partner for her turns out to be her grandfather, a wise Christian philosopher.

David Hein

Acknowledgements

MARGARET CARLISLE CUPIT

It took me a while to begin writing this. It took me too long. Parts of it were too painful to live more than once, better kept locked away in the parts of my memory that only came out when I didn't have control of my mind—in dreams, in waves of emotion, in my most drugged states during chemotherapy treatments. Eventually, though, I decided that I had to start somewhere, because my story was something that I wanted to share. It was something I wanted to use to spread awareness about childhood cancer, about all cancer, and to change things as much as I could. It was, in the most awful of ways, my gift. And so I began to write.

I firmly believe that I wouldn't be alive today if it weren't for the support and love of my family, who stood by me during the most awful of times. Through all the vomit, the anguish, and an often terrible attitude, their love was unfaltering and unconditional

Mama, you were there in every single moment of my experience. You gave me the courage I didn't have, the comfort I needed, and the love that kept me going. You went through my treatment as much as I did, and you did it with far more grace. You are an example that I will always model myself after, an example of selfless love and perfect mothering. I loved our time together throughout my cancer treatment. I loved the laughs you brought me, the hugs you gave me, and your drying the tears from my face. Part of me will always miss those days, because no matter how awful they were, I got to spend time with you.

To my sisters, Sissy and Flynn: Thank you for being there for me in every moment. Whether you were at my bedside or trying your best to get through the school year, I know that I was never alone. Thank you for understanding that I needed Mama to be there with me even when you needed her too. Thank you for keeping me entertained on the boring days. Thank you for holding my hand, for making me laugh, and for supplying me with the memories that kept me going and the motivation to continue living so I could be your sister. Thank you for remembering the funny things I said in chemo that I didn't remember later and for bringing them up just to see me smile. Thank you for never treating me differently just because I was a cancer patient and for always treating me like the middle child I am. You are my best friends in the world, and I will always owe you for the support, patience, and courage you gave me.

Paul, thank you for keeping our lives intact while we weren't around to do it. You took care of the dogs and the house and still found time to work and visit us often. Thanks for taking care of the whole family, for being strong when we could not, for being the glue that held us together through it all.

Anne, thank you for being the perfect "babysitter" and for spoiling me with hugs, snuggling, and good movies. Throughout my journey with cancer, I enjoyed the time we had to be together and get to know each other even more, and I greatly benefitted from all your psychological insight. I have always been able to count on you for everything—love, advice, and support when I was most in danger of falling.

To the staff at St. Jude: Thank you for taking such good care of me, emotionally as well as physically. Thank you for helping me to get well and for inspiring me to follow in your footsteps one day.

Dr. Greer, thank you for your friendship and your comfort. Thank you for becoming part of my family and an even bigger part of my heart.

To my friends, both pre-cancer and post-cancer: Thank you for sticking by me during the hardest period of my life and for giving me something to look forward to when I got well and for understanding when I wasn't feeling myself. You have been with me through the worst of times; this is what it means to be a true friend. For those of you I did not know until after my cure, thank you for helping me fully heal into the full person I believe I have become once again. Thank you for accepting me, for supporting me, for embracing me in my journey back to "normalcy"—or something like it.

To Uncle Carlisle, Nini, Andy Andrews, Sam Martin, and Lisa Anderson: Thank you for helping me with my issues of faith, with the spiritual aspects of this journey when I was unsure of what and how to believe. You made me want to keep searching for hope and for the Divine, and I will carry your lessons with me forever.

To all of my St. Jude Friends: Thank you for letting me lean on you, and thank you for leaning on me. I am so thankful for your understanding and your friendship. Keep fighting and never give up.

To Dr. William Troutt, Mel Richie, and the rest of the Rhodes College staff: Thank you for helping to make St. Jude an option for me and for making my transition in and out of college as smooth as possible. Thank you for your support, kindness, and the wealth of opportunities that you provided me with at Rhodes College.

To Odie Mason Harris: Odie, wherever you are—somewhere in heaven, on a cloud, or maybe even right beside me—know that you will always be my angel and my inspiration. I will never forget you, and I will never forget the promises I made to you.

To Drew: Thank you for always listening to the details of "my story," with compassion and understanding, no matter how many times you have had to hear it. Thank you for asking questions and wanting to know the hardest parts without ever being afraid. Thank you for choosing to get close to me despite my nuanced past, but most of all, thank you for helping to bring me into the present with hope for a long and happy future.

Last, but not least, to Grandpapa: Thank you for believing in my words and in my message, for helping me to make something beautiful from my days of trouble, and for guiding me to the light. Thank you for your hard work on this project, for your labor of love. I am so honored to be your granddaughter and coauthor.

EDWARD HUGH HENDERSON

Bringing Maggie's story to print is my gift to her and to her family, especially to her mother Ellie and sisters Anne Houston and Flynn. It has been a thoroughly enjoyable experience for me. But the gift was produced mostly by Maggie's own deep experience and creativity, making the book a gift *to* me more than a gift *from* me. As a gift from Maggie it has enabled Nini and me to know her and to be more part of her and her family's life than we would have been without it. How mysterious it is that something as terrible as cancer and the torturous treatment it requires should have the benefits that Maggie's cancer has had!

Although this is decidedly not a work in philosophical theology, my effort to address Maggie's concerns about faith and to comment on her experience grow out of the ways I have learned from philosophers and theologians to think about matters of faith. I am grateful to many and would like to mention especially Austin Farrer and Diogenes Allen, who are deceased, and Robert Sokolowski and Richard Rohr. They are not responsible for the uses I have made of their ideas.

It is impossible to give adequate thanks to St. Jude Children's Research Hospital and its physicians, nurses, therapists, chaplains, and staff for the kind of care they provide. To visit this place that is St. Jude is to experience wise love operating efficiently. Maggie's caregivers are named in the book, but let me also name some others associated with Maggie's treatment at St. Jude. These include William Evans, recently retired director and CEO of St. Jude, whom Maggie was honored to introduce as the baccalaureate speaker at Rhodes College last May. Richard Shadyac and Marlo Thomas, through the American, Lebanese, and Syrian Associated Charities (ALSAC), gave Maggie some wonderful experiences speaking for St. Jude in different places and meeting many people in different parts of the country.

Thanks of course go to my daughter, Maggie's mother, Eleanor (Ellie) Phillips. Maggie calls you her "hero." That goes for me, too. You were an amazing source of strength and stability for Maggie and for the rest of us during the year of her treatment, all the while more terrified than the rest of us because of what you knew and experienced every day. But all the family was there as needed: sisters Anne Houston (Sissy) and Flynn, stepfather Paul, uncle Carlisle, grandmother Anne, and father Malcolm and stepmother Marlene.

There were also others whose actions behind the scenes made it possible for Maggie to be treated at St. Jude and who gave her different kinds of support while she was there: William Troutt, president of Rhodes College, and his wife Carole, Rick and Laila Eckles, Melanie and Warren Richey, and Greer and Carol Richardson, all part of the Rhodes College community who befriended and helped Maggie and her family in both known and unknown ways.

I would also mention those who partner with St. Jude Children's Research Hospital to provide housing for patients and their families. For Maggie these are the Memphis Grizzlies basketball team for sponsoring Grizzly House and the Target Corporation for sponsoring Target Houses I and II. There are also Tri Delta Place, sponsored by the Tri Delta Fraternity, and Ronald McDonald House, sponsored by the McDonald's Corporation. Because of your gifts to St. Jude, Maggie and her mother and sister were able to live comfortably and be close by when problems requiring immediate attention arose. There are also thousands around the world who donate to St. Jude. All donations, small and large, have their roots in the kingdom of heaven. The Cupit, Phillips, and Henderson families thank you.

Thanks are also due to the CaringBridge website for providing Maggie and countless other sufferers a way to track their experience and to receive messages of loving concern from a wide network of friends and well-wishers. It's a wonderful service.

My friend David Hein, with whom I have happily worked on other projects, also helped me with this one. David, I am amazed at how quickly you respond to my questions and at how well you can identify particular points that need attention. Students who benefit from your writing instruction cannot possibly appreciate the level of help they receive. But I appreciate it and am once again much in your debt.

Portions of this book were read to the "Lunch with C. S. Lewis" program for students at St. Alban's Chapel and Student Center at LSU and to a program of the Center for Spiritual Formation of St. James Episcopal Church in Baton Rouge. The enthusiastic responses and the lively discussions we enjoyed encouraged me in the belief that this book would be useful to others, which in turn shaped the way Maggie and I presented it.

Thanks are due to Highland Coffees and to Garden District Coffee for the civilized working conditions they provided. I also thank the Department of Philosophy and Religious Studies and the College of Humanities and Social Sciences at The Louisiana State University for providing me with the tools of writing. The religious views expressed herein are by no means to be attributed to them.

I reserve my deepest gratitude for my wife Tricia and for my granddaughter Maggie. Tricia appears in the book as "Nini," the name by which she is affectionately called by Maggie and her sisters.

Tricia, you have given me every encouragement over the course of my career and now in the first two years of retirement the time needed to get the work done. You have joyfully joined the writing process, spent hours reading, evaluating, and constructively critiquing the organization and the content of the book. More than that, your wisdom gave direction to it. I am thankful we have been able to work on this project together. Just as important, your prayerful life has had more of a steering effect and benefit for me than you can possibly know.

And Maggie, your journal, kept in the middle of your suffering, gave your family and friends a way to share life with you and to help you bear the burden (Gal 6:2). When I was a student at Rhodes (then Southwestern-at-Memphis), philosophy majors were known as "cloud eaters." I guess I have been one most all my life. But your illness and your journal and your willingness to let me write with you about them have enabled me to come down out of the philosophical and theological clouds to find the concrete meaning of the abstractions. Reading and following the spiritual thread and pattern in your journal has changed my thinking. Most importantly, however, the book project has let Nini and me know you as we probably never would have had we not undertaken it.

Introduction

THE MAKING OF THIS BOOK

When my granddaughter Maggie (Margaret Carlisle Cupit) was in treatment for Ewing's Sarcoma, we carried on an email "faith conversation." Maggie had many questions about God and did not think of herself as having faith. I thought our exchange could be made into a useful article for a semi-popular religious magazine, something for clergy and intellectually inclined lay people who might be interested in discussions of the problem of suffering and evil. However, as I read and reread the journal Maggie kept as she went through treatment, I lost interest in turning our email conversation into such an article: better to place Maggie's experience in the foreground, for her journal unfolds and describes an authentic journey of faith as she wrestled through physical, psychological, and spiritual suffering. Instead of a scholarly piece, I decided to present the substance of her journey in a form that could inspire and strengthen the spiritual lives of others whose life circumstances lead them also to ask the "Why, God?" question. I would devote myself to Maggie's experience. I would arrange and comment on her journal and recollections. I would track and try to lay bare the spiritual or faith dimensions of her journey through cancer treatment. I dare to believe that the result helps us to see the hidden, sacramental presence of God and how it is possible in the midst of suffering, even because of suffering, to receive the good for which God has created us.

Let me be emphatic. This book does not try to answer all the questions about suffering and God. It is a practical, not a philosophical response to suffering. It offers a way of living through suffering rather than answers to philosophical questions. But it does have an intellectual side. It presents a way of seeing God's action in the world that differs from the common view that God plans and so causes everything, including cancer and other causes of suffering and death, and from the companion view that blames God for not acting to eliminate all suffering.

The book combines two things. First, there is the journal by a nineteen-year-old college student written in the throes of a regimen of brutal chemotherapy. And, second, there is the commentary of a grandfather who is a retired teacher of philosophy of religion and who also tries to be a faithful Christian. I hope that readers struggling with the reality of suffering and death will find here that it is possible to take the "Why, God?" question seriously and in facing it find help for their souls.

Maggie's encounter with deadly disease is not unique. Disease, painful medical treatments, mental illness, harmful accidents, floods, landslides, fires, tornados, hurricanes, poverty, hunger, betrayals, hatred, murder, war—the world is full of terrible things. It also contains many persons who make faithful responses to the suffering life brings them. We are justified in singling out Maggie's experience of suffering, not because it is unique but because she lived faithfully through it and has written perceptively, beautifully, and helpfully about it.

Love is at the center of this book, but 'love' is a dangerous word. It is used far too loosely in our time. Yet no other word will quite do the job. I am going to trust that Maggie's journal and the accompanying commentary will prevent misunderstanding. And I must explain that I think Plato was right in his *Symposium* when he had Socrates argue that "desire" is the essential core of love. Some theologians have thought that God's self-giving love cannot involve desire because desire, as Socrates argued, seeks that which it lacks. Since, they say, God's perfection lacks nothing, God cannot have desire. I disagree with that view. Divine love does involve desire, but it is a desire that flows from the complete fullness and perfection of love that is God. Divine love is the holy desire to share the joy of the life of perfect love. When we say that God desires that we share in the life of perfect love, we do not imply that our failures to love diminish the perfection of the life of love that God enjoys.

The first and second commandments are inextricably mingled. To love God is to desire what God desires. God desires that we love God and our neighbors. Therefore, if we love our neighbors, we love God—whether we know it or not—because loving our neighbors is doing what God desires us to do. And if we do not love our neighbors, then we do not love

God because we do not do what God desires us to do. When we desire the real good of others and are made happy when it is fulfilled for them, then, whether we know it or not, we are living and experiencing the action of God in ourselves. So, Maggie came to recognize God in the love she received and in the love she gave.

The experience of genuine love is the springing point of lived faith. Authentic religious life grows this experience of love in the life of persons. It grows from there into the beliefs, traditions, and practices which tell persons how the world is and how life is best to be lived so as to express and extend the love from which it comes. It goes without saying, however, that religious beliefs and practices are often used for other purposes and that these other uses can amount to misuse. Maggie's difficulties with religion derive from the observation of such misuse.

Things have thus far worked out so well for Maggie that it is tempting to think (and numerous people have told me this) that the cancer must have been "part of God's plan" for her. Maggie and I disagree with them. We do not believe that God plans to give some persons terrible diseases or hit them with terrible calamities while sparing others, and we do not believe God plans to cause some to be cured and others to die painful and untimely deaths. That is not, we think, the kind of "planning" God does for God's creatures.

Most people most of the time, I believe, think that the threads in the fabric of the world are both loose enough and regular enough for chance, for choice, and for some degree of personal responsibility. If every event in life were determined by an eternal divine plan, there would be no room for chance or choice and no room for personal responsibility. Worse still, since forced love is not real love at all, there would be no room for the love of God and neighbor. The world God has planned must surely have been planned to be the kind of world in which real love can exist and grow.

There is always a faithful response to be made to disease and disaster, and to all events that bring suffering. Faithful responses lead to outcomes that often make us think that all the events leading to good outcomes must be part of God's "plan." St. Paul was wise in saying that God works all things into good for those who love God (Rom 8:28). For when we love God and respond faithfully to the circumstances of life, then we receive more of the good God most desires us to have, the-good-no-matter-what. That good, however, is not necessarily the elimination of our suffering or the fulfillment of our various desires; it is the good God desires that we should have now and always.

There is a difference between God's *acting in our faithful responses to bring good out of bad things*, on the one hand, and God's *causing bad things to happen as a means to good ends*, on the other. The good God desires most for us to have is that we become full participants in the divine life of perfect love, that we become persons who love God with all our hearts, with all our minds, with all our souls, and with all our strength—and that we love our neighbors as ourselves. Maggie's faithful response to the cancer was to recognize and receive the love offered to her and to return love to others as well. Thus, God worked good through Maggie's response to her pain and suffering. So it is that God accomplishes God's plan for faithful persons, not by afflicting them with suffering in order to accomplish the plan, but by acting in and through their faithful actions of love.

And what if Maggie's treatment had been unsuccessful? Would we now be saying that God had worked good in the events of her cancer treatment? Given that Maggie described the good she experienced as in some way a good that is outside of time and as good no matter what, our answer should be "Yes." And the example of her friend Odie shows that one can receive the good God intends for us even if one comes to an early death because the cure does not work. Did God plan for Odie to get an incurable cancer and to die at age thirteen? I do not believe so. But Odie responded faithfully to his intractable disease in the way that was possible for him. That is not to say that he responded in sophisticated theological thought-forms. He did not. But he responded with grace and love in a spirit of gratitude for his life and for the people in it. We can see through the sadness of his untimely death to the value of his life, and we can give thanks for him and for his friendship with Maggie.

On the other hand, we know of persons who have been cured of their disease and who nevertheless have been bitter and angry, often complaining of the terrible things inflicted upon them and of the pain they have had to endure. They become less grateful for their healing and less able to enjoy the people from whom they might have accepted love and to whom they might have returned it. They sink into angry bitterness and self-pity over the suffering and the uncertainty with which they must live. They diminish the good God desires to give them.

Can authentically faithful persons believe that God directly intends death, disease, and disaster in order to accomplish good? Of course they can. Not all persons who strive to be faithful are going to think the same way, and they do not have to in order to be faithful. Perhaps most believers over the centuries have used just such a rationale to rationalize the presence of suffering in a world created by a good God. The point to remember here is that how one thinks about God and God's ways with the world is not the most important part of the life of faith. The most important part is the living relationship of the faithful to God: in love, trust, obedience, and hope. There are many ways to think, and many of them (I do not say "all") are compatible with a faithful relationship with God. As Richard Rohr likes to say, God does not command that we get our theological ideas right; God commands that we love God and our neighbors.[3] Nevertheless, it is true that the way we think will affect the way we relate to God, and that is why the intellectual aspect one brings to or is able to adopt in the experience of suffering is important.

There is no question but that life is far more difficult for some than for others. Some are born into circumstances in which the possibility of experiencing love has been extinguished at the outset. There are some, perhaps many, for whom a faithful response to suffering just may be impossible. We must trust in the ultimate mercy of God.

Edward Henderson

READING THIS BOOK

The initials MCC are used in the headings to identify Margaret Carlisle Cupit (Maggie) as the author of journal entries and recollections. The initials EHH identify her grandfather Edward Hugh Henderson as the author of email messages (in chapters 4 and 5) and comments throughout.

MCC has two kinds of contributions in the book: journal entries, which were written as she was going through treatment at St. Jude, and recollections, which were written either in the summer of 2011 after the treatments were completed or in the summer of 2014 when she graduated from Rhodes College and was looking back over her experience. The precise dates of the journal entries are given in the headings, while the later recollections are marked by the month and year they were written. The book follows a dramatic and chronological order. Thus, recollections written in the summer after Maggie's year at St. Jude have been placed with the journal entries written contemporaneously with the events to which they

---

3. Rohr, *Things Hidden*, 37–39.

both refer. The chronological order is the order of Maggie's experience, not always precisely the order of her writing about it.

The contributions by EHH are only dated in chapters 4 and 5, where they consist of email messages that fit into the chronology of Maggie's story and whose dates are known. His other contributions are commentary on the story as it is told through MCC's journal and recollections.

Chapters 2, 3, 9 (and all but the last paragraph of chapter 10) are entirely by Maggie. The story is hers.

The Hard Rocks of Reality

MCC, JUNE, 2011

My freshman year at Rhodes College was glorious, the happiest year I had ever had, the most challenging, most provocative, and the most fruitful. I learned how to solve differential equations, how to rationally explain my vegetarianism, and how to write a college paper. I learned how to titrate acids and bases, how to read ancient texts, and how to write a short story. I learned why the sugar trade was important to Great Britain and slavery, why Gandhi had such an effect on his people, and why Christianity spread so quickly. I began to learn who I was, what a true friend looked like, and how truly inspiring a college professor could be. I gained a few pounds, a hundred friendships, and twenty role models. I acted out Sophocles' plays in the amphitheater, helped win a ninth-place trophy at Mock Trial Nationals, and journeyed to the top of Palmer Hall to talk and eat cookies with my very English professor who taught me British Literature. I held a work-study position in the college president's office where I actually got to know the president of the college, won the freshman chemistry award, made a 4.0, and was selected for a research fellowship at St. Jude Children's Research Hospital. Overwhelmed with success and excitement, I emailed my Grandpapa, a Rhodes graduate himself, to tell him that I loved Rhodes so much that I wished I could stay there forever. But on what should have been my first day as a research fellow at St. Jude, I found myself as a patient there instead, beginning chemotherapy for a life-threatening form of bone cancer called Ewing's sarcoma. Nearly four years have passed, and although I have a titanium tibia and knee as well as a fierce battle scar from my thigh to my ankle, I am healthy—free of cancer. I am graduating from Rhodes College, and I will begin medical school in the fall in hopes of becoming a pediatric oncologist. My life is rich. Filled with excitement for my future, I am content.

My battle with cancer, however, was not one of contentment, for there were always questions running through my mind. Why me? What did I do to deserve cancer? If children and babies, the least deserving, get cancer, then where is God? Why does God let that happen? Does God cause cancer? Does everything happen for a reason? Do people die long, painful deaths after tons of miserable chemo because God wants them to, because that is God's plan for them? Sometimes I felt like God was too far away from everything I was experiencing, that surely God didn't care about me if he'd allowed cancer to happen to me.

I began praying the moment I found out cancer was a possibility. While I would like to say my urge to pray was a result of my faith, it is likely that it was a result of my upbringing and desperation. I clung to God because God was the only one who could change my diagnosis. "Don't let it be cancer. Please, don't let it be cancer, God. I know you wouldn't let that happen to me. I have too many plans." I thought that things would go back to normal soon, that I would wake up from the terrible nightmare I was having and resume a normal life. I never did wake up, and gradually I realized that I was inside of my actual life, not inside of a dream. God did not step in and reverse my diagnosis.

I've always had doubts. I can't remember an age when I didn't question my faith, at least from time to time. I've never been good at pushing thoughts away or hiding them. I've been curious for my whole life, and I've always asked a lot of questions. These things haven't made faith easy for me. Still, though, I have always yearned for a spiritual connection and searched for religious affirmation, unable to abandon such a quest of utmost importance and unable to give up on believing or looking for the answers to my questions. When I received the diagnosis, however, and when I began cancer treatment and everything that came with it, my faith was shaken as never before.

I could have given up on God and the idea of God, but I didn't. It wasn't fear that kept me from closing off my mind to the possibility of God.

In my mind, giving up on God without a thorough search was just as silly as believing in God without a thorough search.

EHH

My granddaughter Maggie's diagnosis and treatment for Ewing's sarcoma pressed questions about God and God's ways with the world, pressed them on Maggie, of course, but also on those who love her. With encouragement and input from Tricia, my wife and Maggie's step-grandmother (Maggie knows her as Nini, and she will be so named hereafter), I proposed a "faith conversation," which Maggie and I could conduct mainly through email and on Nini's and my occasional trips to Memphis to visit her at St. Jude Children's Research Hospital.

Even as our faith conversation was taking place, it became clear to me that Maggie's growth in faith had far more to do with the painful and frightening experience she was going through than with abstract theological thinking. Maggie (and her family and friends) had run into the hard rocks of reality. This collision made Maggie's experience a most important part of her search for God. By the time she was able to return to college more than a year later, she had suffered both physical and mental pain, lived through the deaths of several young friends, and faced the possibility of her own early death.

Maggie had not expected that the search for God would be so much like science. As science only advances when hypotheses are tested against stubborn facts, so it is with matters of the spirit. No faith in God can advance unless its beliefs are tested against the stubborn facts of life. For Maggie, cancer became the fact against which the search for God and for faith to trust God would have to go forward. Only in this case the stubborn fact is not one from which one can gain objective distance as one might from facts in a lab; nor can one come to a conclusion that might be accepted by all. In this case the "proof" involves one in an ongoing act of courage and commitment.

As she suffered through the hard realities of a year of cancer treatment, Maggie was embedded in a wealth of relationships. These included a new and deeper relationship with family and friends, especially with her mother, her two sisters, her stepfather, her grandmother, her uncle, and with Nini and me. Beyond these newly shaped relationships with her immediate family are the relationships that developed with the doctors, nurses, therapists, others on the St. Jude staff, an Episcopal priest, and, most powerfully, with other patients; for it was with these young fellow-sufferers that Maggie confronted the pain, the uncertainty, the possibility, and, for some, the reality of death.

These relationships became the matrix within which Maggie was nurtured and sustained as she suffered into faith. The term "matrix" is important. A matrix is literally a womb, which is a living system of interacting members through which something new is brought to life, not simply as the passive recipient of causally inflicted effects, but as a living agent actively receiving and using the nurture provided in the matrix and in turn reciprocally affecting the other members. As Maggie suffers into faith, those around her find themselves also suffering and growing. But this is Maggie's story. The focus will be on her.

We will enter into Maggie's story with what she wrote in the summer of 2011 when her year of chemotherapy and surgery was over and she had been declared "cancer free." These reflections will be followed by selections from her CaringBridge journal and by emails constituting the "faith conversation" Maggie and I carried on. These emails and journal entries were written in the midst of the physical pain and mental anguish of treatment, when she did not know what was coming next or what the outcome was to be. It is in them that we best see the working of the matrix: the relationships with family, friends, and therapists, the theological questioning and thinking, and the relationships with the other patients and their families. In this working we will see Maggie suffering into faith.

One of the things the journal entries will show is the enormous role other patients play in Maggie's spiritual growth. Maggie found herself going out to them and in this powerful thing that was happening to her she began to sense and then to know that her wound was sacred. As she began to see God in her fellow sufferers, she was able to see meaning in the suffering, to find that God was in it and with her cooperation would make it count for good, and this without seeing God as intentionally causing her to have cancer as part of some detailed divine plan for her life. Maggie's faith was not structured by particular doctrines of Christian theology, but she came to see the effective presence of God, especially in the lives of the people around her, and to know that the matrix in which she lived was in fact the hidden kingdom of God.

But philosophical and theological thinking are also at work in the matrix. Thinking, questioning, wondering, doubting, receiving and weighing ideas, responding, seeing new ways to understand, even appreciating the limits of every way of thinking and the limits of all ideas: these are part of life. Such inclusion in life does not in itself negate thought's ability to know truly. In Maggie's case, I believe that the thinking she did in her writing and in dialog with others was helpful in removing obstacles to faith and helping her to form a faith that is able to include doubt and different ways of understanding without making faith into a fearful adherence to comforting beliefs. Such faith, I believe, allows one to trust in and depend on God rather than on doctrines.

As we follow Maggie through the year of her treatment and attend to her reflections, we see God at work forming and transforming, doing what C. S. Lewis called "surgery" on her soul.[1] By the eve of her return to college life, we find Maggie affirming a faith that has made friends with doubt, disappointment, and uncertainty while declaring hope that the mysterious God intends good for us and can be trusted to accomplish it even through suffering and death. This is by no means to say that Maggie, any more than the rest of us, is a finished product. Maggie's epilogue, written just after her graduation from Rhodes College, shows that her life of faith continues to seek understanding even as she continues to intersect with ever new facets of reality.

The diagnosis came in mid-May 2010; the first treatment came shortly after. It was in the setting of that suffering that Maggie faced in an intensely concrete way the questions philosophers of religion discuss in distant and abstract ways. Let the questioning and answering unfold in the telling of her story. It all began in the spring semester of her first year at Rhodes College . . .

---

1. Lewis, *Till We Have Faces*, 253–54.

2

But I Have Plans

MCC, JUNE, 2011

He looked down at the papers on his lap. "It looks like there is some abnormal tissue in your leg."

How did I get to that point? How did my normal, seemingly perfect life turn into something else? How did my biggest worry go from making good grades to surviving? Had I done something wrong? How had God let this happen to me? These were questions for which I had no answers. I guess I'll just start from the beginning.

I had just finished the most exciting half-year of my entire eighteen years of life: my first semester of college. If you think it was because of the alcohol and freedom, you're wrong. I had never had a drink in my life. I was the type of person who loved college because of my two biggest life passions: people and learning. College happened to be full of both things. For me, college was my idea of heaven. I had a high GPA, a dozen best friends, and, for the first time in my life, a fully stimulated mind. Rhodes College was the perfect place for me in every way possible.

Halfway through that first year, the pain started. While I was visiting a college friend and her family over winter break in Rhode Island, my right knee began to throb. I didn't think anything of it. After all, I had just taught a yoga session to the whole family that morning, right in front of the Christmas tree. Yes, I was a bit of a show-off, and I had worked extra hard to demonstrate my yoga abilities, so I figured I had just pulled a muscle or was extra sore. I took some ibuprofen and waited. When we watched a movie later that night, I couldn't take my mind off the pain in my leg long enough to focus. The next day, I woke up in pain. I continued to take ibuprofen, which worked for the time being.

I don't remember exactly how many days went by between then and the next time my leg started hurting, but it was long enough for me to lose track of time. Let me make one thing clear: I have never been much of an athlete. I tried to make myself exercise to stay somewhat in shape during my freshman year, and my exercise routine usually entailed a mile or two of fast-paced uphill walking followed by a mile of running. I would do yoga when I felt like it, but it was often for relaxation rather than physical fitness. On this particular day, I noticed that running the mile was incredibly difficult, even more difficult than usual. "It must have been a really long time since my last run," I thought to myself as I walked to the water cooler across the gym, struggling to make it across the room. As I walked back across campus through the cold, I pulled a sweatshirt over my sweaty head and cringed from the pain in my leg. I blamed the pain on the pulled muscle I never got checked out, made it back to my room, and took an ibuprofen. I turned on the shower to let the water heat up and began undressing in the mirror. As I scanned my body, I noticed that my right knee was slightly bigger than my left.

The pain went away after a few days, and I forgot all about it. A few weeks later, my mock trial team headed to Missouri for a regional tournament. We loaded the van excitedly, and I began practicing my characters, complete with accents, as soon as we left the parking lot. After a few hours, I noticed that my leg felt like it needed stretching. This made sense; we'd been driving without any stops. Not too much later, we stopped for a bathroom break somewhere between Memphis and St. Louis. It was one of those little towns off the highway, most likely populated by a few mountain people. As I climbed out of the van to stretch my legs, I felt my leg begin to throb again. I sighed aloud, frustrated with what had become a continuous problem.

"My leg hurts really bad," I said to my friend Katherine.

"I'm sorry, baby. Did you take anything?"

"Not yet. But lately nothing helps," I whined.

Katherine squeezed my shoulders and gave me a big, comforting hug. She always knew the right thing to say and do. She was a nurturer, a mother to everyone around her, despite the fact that she deserved to be nurtured more than anyone I have ever met. She told me to try Aleve. I hadn't tried that yet, so later that night, after rehearsal and dinner I bought a bottle at a drug store on our way back to the hotel. By the time we got ready for bed, though, the pain wasn't gone at all. It was elevated. I called my mother, complaining, and she told me to calm down. I began crying. I was on the verge of panic.

"I need to see a doctor," I said forcefully, through the blur of tears streaming down my face.

"Calm down, Maggie. Please just make it through this weekend. You can't make your mock trial team go to the emergency room right now. You'll ruin the tournament for everyone."

Later that night, as I lay in bed with Katherine, I began crying again. To this day, I cannot remember having pain that intense, even after my leg surgery. That night was the most painful thing I have ever experienced. I began shaking and sweating because there was nothing else I could do. I couldn't sleep, and no matter how many massages Katherine gave me to calm me down, I became hysterical. Katherine promised me it would be okay and held my hand. She told me to squeeze it whenever I had pain, as hard as I needed to. I remember staying up all night, squeezing her hand way after she had fallen asleep, even getting up in the middle of the night and taking a hot bath in efforts to soothe my leg. The bath did nothing for me. In fact, it frustrated me even more. It was hard for me to get in and out of the tub with my leg. The next morning, it was a rainy day. I put on my high heels and limped downstairs.

"Are you limping?" my coach said.

"Yes, sir. My leg has been hurting and I'm not sure why. I think maybe I tore a tendon or a ligament or something. I'm okay, though."

I was lying; I was not okay. I felt like someone was hitting my leg with a hammer. I thought about the people in those *Saw* movies, the people who endure all kinds of physical torture. I compared myself to them. At that point, my theory had changed. The pain was too severe for a pulled muscle. I picked up my cell phone and called my mom. I told her how severe the pain had been and that I had been tempted to go to the emergency room due to its severity. She told me that she was so glad I had not made my "poor mock trial coach" go to the emergency room in the middle of the night. The rest of the trip was not easy, by any means, but the pain never got as bad as it had that first night. I spent the tournament limping around in the extra pair of shoes I was forced to bring so that I wasn't in my high heels the entire time. When it was time for me to take my place on the witness stand, I clenched my teeth, put on a fake smile, and forced myself to walk normally.

As a team, we did really well and qualified for the next rounds leading up to nationals. I was relieved I had made it through the tournament. As soon as I got back to school, I called my mom and scheduled an appointment with an orthopedist for my next trip home—spring break.

In the weeks leading up to spring break, my leg occasionally swelled up, which was not a problem. It throbbed from time to time, which was a problem, but for that I had IcyHot. Every time my leg hurt, and as long as I wasn't in public, I would slather my entire right leg in that pungent sticky stuff, hoping that it would give me some relief. It didn't do much, to be honest, but it was the only thing that helped at all. I even took it with me on the next mock trial trip. This trip was to nationals, held on our own turf, in Memphis, but we stayed on the other side of town from Rhodes, so we couldn't be "distracted." I thought my roommates on that trip would be leery of my using such a strong-smelling concoction on my leg, but they were very understanding. One of the girls was apparently a huge fan of IcyHot. She told me she loved it and had used it often when she played sports in high school. I was glad to share with her and watched in amazement as she slathered it on her arms and legs. Looking back, I feel sorry for the other girl who roomed with us that weekend. Every time we came back into the hotel room, we were welcomed by the strong and powerful, yet very recognizable scent of IcyHot. I'm sure the scent of IcyHot will always bring memories of my days of undiagnosed leg pain.

The national tournament was held downtown in the Memphis courthouse and spread out inside a few large, brick buildings. Downtown Memphis does not offer much parking, so, unfortunately for me, this meant I had to do a good bit of walking around in my pink high heels that weekend. I braced myself for a very long and somewhat painful weekend, but I persevered because of dedication to my mock trial teammates. Of course, my passion for pretending to be a Mississippi pageant queen with an exaggerated Southern accent did not hurt.

Our team had a tradition of exiting the courtroom a few minutes before the trial began, in order to enjoy a pep talk and dance the hokey pokey. As we danced the hokey pokey before the first round, I noticed how hard it was for me to put my right leg in and out of the circle. It was even harder to shake it and dance around on it. This concerned me, but I told myself that I didn't need to panic. There was nothing to worry about, right?

The last round of nationals came, and my leg began to hurt. I was miserable, changing positions over and over again, limping around in an attempt to stretch. And then my parents arrived. Relieved, I limped over to my mother.

"Something bad is wrong with my leg, Mama."

She looked at me with a look of sympathy and gave me a hug.

"It's alright, honey. I'm sure it's nothing serious. Stop worrying about it."

I could tell from the look in her face that she thought I was complaining for attention, that it was an act just like my witness. "She and everyone else," I thought. As the round began, the pain in my leg flared up again, and I tried to be still, not wanting to draw attention to myself. That seemed to make things even worse. Finally, my name was called. Actually, it wasn't my name. It was "Sydney Melana Michaels," the name of my witness in the case. I took a deep breath, smiled, and pushed myself forward to the witness stand, striving to walk normally and with a little attitude. I'm sure I was limping a little at that point.

Our team did well, extremely well. We attended the awards ceremony downtown and received a ninth-place trophy. We were pleased, and the next week the pain in my leg seemed to fade yet again. It was time to go home for spring break.

While I was home, I had an appointment with an orthopedist. He was a very kind man, and we hit it off immediately. He knew someone who had graduated from Rhodes College, and he was impressed when I told him that I had been selected to participate in a research program at St. Jude Children's Research Hospital. He examined my leg as I explained to him that the pain had been severe but had gone away. He ordered an X-Ray. The X-Ray was short and easy, and my mother and I returned again a few days later to get the results. I was a little nervous because I knew that I had torn something and didn't want to have to have surgery during the summer because of my research position. When we saw the doctor, though, he smiled, and I sighed in relief. He greeted me with a hug like we were old friends and sat down to tell my mother and me that the X-Ray showed nothing abnormal.

"It was really hurting, though," I said, a little confused.

"If it was serious, then the X-Ray would have picked it up. You may have just pulled a muscle."

I thought about thanking him, standing up, and leaving the room. But something else held me there.

"I don't know. I never did anything to hurt it. Are you sure?"

He looked up at me and said, "We can do an MRI just to be sure if you want."

We agreed to do just that a few weeks later when I planned to return home for Easter break. That never happened, though. Easter came along, and I decided not to go home, even though I needed to get my leg checked out. Instead, I went home to Dallas to stay with a couple of friends. One of my friends wore a leg brace the entire trip because she'd hurt her leg playing sports. She was extremely athletic and beautiful, and I was a little jealous when all the cute boys we ran into shopping kept hitting on her. They would say things like, "What did you do to your leg?" or "Oh yeah, I hurt my leg a while back so I know how you feel."

"What about me?" I thought selfishly. After all, my leg was hurting too.

After limping to several of my final exams, it was time to go home for the summer, and I wasn't ready. I didn't want the year to end. I said goodbye to my friend Macie and told her that I would see her soon because she had plans to be at my house a few days later, on her way home from school to New Orleans.

By the time Macie arrived, I had had the MRI and it was time to pick up the results. Since my mom was still teaching school, Macie went with me to Hattiesburg. We waited in the waiting room, and I occupied myself with some free coffee. I didn't realize it, but that was the last time I would drink coffee for quite some time.

I knew that something was wrong the moment the doctor came into the examining room. He wasn't smiling, and he didn't greet me with a hug as he had before. He avoided eye contact and pulled up a stool on wheels. He sat down very slowly. You could've heard a pin drop. I stared out the window at the pine trees and waited.

It felt like minutes went by while I stared out the window and the doctor tried to find the courage to speak, the courage to know what to say. Finally, I spoke up. "What's wrong with my leg?"

He looked down at the papers on his lap. "It looks like there is some abnormal tissue in your leg."

Too many thoughts ran through my mind. Used alone, the words "abnormal" and "tissue" seemed like nothing to worry about. Together, though, especially when applied to me, they made my heart fall into my stomach. I looked back outside, at the small forest of pine trees, at the gray roof of the floors below us, at the cars driving by, and I asked, "Is it cancer?"

"That is a possibility," he said, ripping the sentence into pieces, letting one word fall out of his mouth at a time. I knew by the way he looked at me when his eyes met mine that it was more than a possibility. It was a diagnosis. He already knew that there was cancer in my body. He just didn't know how much.

We waited in that room for two and a half hours for my family to drive down. At first, I just sat there for a few minutes. I looked at Macie, and she looked terrified, but she told me that it was probably not cancer and that the doctor just had to say that to be honest about every possibility there was. After a while, though, sitting in that quiet doctor's office with the white walls and big window, my decision to be calm went out the window. Tears began to roll down my face. I became louder and louder until I was hysterical, and a nurse came into the room to calm me down. She gave me a hug, which didn't help because it started to seem like everyone in that office knew that I was the girl with the cancer in my leg. What were people saying about me? I asked for a drink, and I took a few sips of Diet Coke, but it didn't help either. They offered me food, but I was already nauseous. I started pacing the room and crying even more. I begged Macie to read me a children's book that I found in the corner of the room atop a stack of parenting magazines, a Berenstain Bears story. She was amazingly calm, and I put my head in her lap and listened to her read to me as we waited for my family to arrive.

By the time they got there, I was in denial. I had stopped crying and just stared at the wall. When the doctor came in to join us, I went to the restroom to throw up. Later, I found out what he told my family while I was gone. He told them that there was cancer in my leg, that there was so much of it there that it was probably all over my body, and that it was probably just a matter of "making me comfortable."

Mama kept crying. I told her to stop crying and that I would be okay. I told her that it probably wasn't cancer after all. My boyfriend at the time said that if it was cancer then I wouldn't even need chemotherapy, just a quick surgery. I believed him. I needed to believe that.

For three days I sat at home and waited for an appointment with an oncologist in New Orleans. Macie and the boyfriend were both staying at my house, and we went swimming during the day. During those three days, I think I noticed the sun more. I think I appreciated it more. I swam around in the pool like a little kid and ate whatever I wanted. I didn't worry about how my hair looked or if I looked fat in my swimsuit. As the sun came in through the window over my bed in the mornings, I wondered if all of it was really happening. I closed my eyes and told myself to wake up, to end the nightmare. I tried to imagine myself with cancer, and I couldn't. So I came to the conclusion that I didn't have cancer. I wasn't feeling sick, after all. Didn't people with cancer feel sick? Still, I prayed harder than I ever had before.

Three days after receiving the MRI results we went to New Orleans to see an oncologist at Ochsner Hospital. My mother, stepfather, little sister Flynn, grandmother Anne, Uncle Carlisle, step-grandmother Nini, Grand-papa, and my friend Macie were all there to wait with me and to give their support. It was May 16, 2010. Before my appointment with the doctor, I did every test from a CT scan to an X-Ray to an MRI to a PET scan. I walked through a lobby of cancer patients as I held my mother's hand. Then we saw the doctor. He got right to the point, and I thought to myself, "He's used to this. He's used to telling people that they're going to die." He put my MRI up on a screen and pointed something out. "This is the tumor," he said.

So there was a tumor. But that didn't mean that it was the bad kind. I held onto the hope that it was just the kind of tumor that didn't need chemo, the kind that needed a quick surgery. I listened patiently as the doctor identified my tumor as "Ewing's sarcoma," a type of bone cancer. He'd said it. Cancer. I had cancer. I felt myself losing control, slipping into panic.

"I won't have to have chemo for this, will I?" I bravely asked the oncologist, "because I already have plans for the summer." I felt like I could handle cancer as long as I didn't have to get chemo.

"Ewing's sarcoma is typically treated with chemotherapy, radiation, and surgery. The good news is that the tumor in your leg was the only one we found. Ewing's sarcoma grows very quickly. You're lucky it isn't in your lungs by now."

The doctor turned to the door and greeted a young man who, he explained, was a resident helping with my case. I felt slightly violated that I was being used as part of someone's education while I was receiving the news that I had cancer. I briefly imagined myself in this resident's shoes, as a different person with a different life and a different set of cards. I began to cry, and I was told that I would get another X-Ray for a closer look at my leg before the biopsy. As we walked down the hallway, I began to sob loudly. I heard loud noises coming uncontrollably out of my throat, the way they did when I was in pre-school. I couldn't calm down, couldn't get a grip on myself, and couldn't stop screaming. I was screaming. I was having a tantrum in the middle of the hospital. I was not dreaming; this I was sure of.

"It's okay, sweetie," the female X-Ray technician said in a soothing voice.

She looked at me in pity and helped me onto the table. It wasn't "okay." How did she know if I was "okay" or not? She had no idea if I was going to be okay or not, if I was going to live or die. She didn't have cancer. I did. I was the one with cancer. I didn't want to miss my job at St. Jude over the summer, I didn't want to receive chemotherapy, and I didn't want to die. For the first time, I had the realistic realization that all three possibilities were very likely.

Finding out you have cancer is worse than hearing people talk about the world ending in 2012 when the Mayan calendar ends. It's worse than finding out that you made an A-minus in your fiction writing class, the easy class you knew you were the best in. It's worse than the incline part of a really fast roller coaster, the kind where you wait and wait and wait for the hill, for the point of no control. Because when you find out you have cancer, in that moment, you lose every ounce of control you ever thought you had, you face the realest thing you've ever faced, and for the only time in your life, the world stops moving.

I was barely nineteen years old, a sister of two, a daughter of a perfect mother, and full of plans. I had decided to be a doctor at age four. That was the first time I almost lost my life. I don't remember much from that part of my life, except for the smell of the hospital rooms, the texture of hospital gowns, and the look in my mother's eyes that she had again on the day I was diagnosed. It was a look of fear, but also much more than fear. It was like looking into her eyes and seeing every memory we had ever made together. I knew she was thinking that I might die. But I knew that she was also praying, begging God that I wouldn't.

I felt guilty for thinking that my family wouldn't work without me. I was never normal, and I was given hell for that in high school, but I knew that I was, in some way, part of the glue that held my family together. So I knew, for that reason, that I couldn't let myself die yet, because I knew that if I died, in many ways, they would die too. "Research shows that survival depends on the frame of mind," I thought to myself as I promised myself I would try to stay positive and beat this thing called "cancer." I decided right then and there that I was going to try my very best.

Just a month earlier, the guy I was dating at the time had practiced a school presentation in front of me. The presentation was about cancer research and finding new cancer treatments as alternatives to chemotherapy. The boyfriend had explained to me the side effects of chemotherapy and had showed me a picture of a person receiving the treatment. The picture made me shiver. I felt sorry for the cancer patient, disgusted even. The person was pale, bald, emaciated. He or she (I couldn't even tell) looked afraid and barely hanging on to life. The word "chemotherapy" had always reminded me of people like the one in the picture. It had sent a chill down my spine. If only I had known that word would soon become a part of me. It would soon make me think of myself.

The oncologist and resident did a biopsy of the detected tumor in my leg, inserted a double port into my chest, and sent me home. As soon as I was completely conscious, I spoke to Macie. She had been there for my surgery, and she had walked into the surgery prep room with my mother to speak to me beforehand. Apparently, as soon as the anesthesia kicked in, I pointed at an empty IV bag and said, "Someone left their Capri Sun on my bed."

I was told that I'd also announced to everyone that the "cute boy" was going to see me naked. I think I was referring to the resident who assisted with the biopsy. It seemed odd to me that I was sharing a laugh with Macie and my family at a time like that. It seemed odd that I had the ability to laugh the day after I'd been diagnosed with cancer. Still, I welcomed the moments of bliss and was eager to savor them. When the biopsy was over, I was wheeled into the waiting room to meet my family, and they brought me home, but all I remember was waking up at home again.

I woke up in my mother's bed. I was so glad to be back home, so glad to be away from hospitals and X-Ray machines and doctors with bad news. I looked down at my leg and realized that the biopsy had been a bigger procedure than I'd anticipated. Most of my right leg was bandaged and tightly wrapped, and it was very painful. I was shocked to find that I couldn't even walk.

For an entire week, I stayed in my parents' bed (in the only downstairs bedroom). Looking back, I can't really say what thoughts went through my head that week. All I remember is lying in bed, staring at the ceiling, and emailing people at my college to notify them that I could not participate in the St. Jude research program I had been so excited about. I know that I didn't cry, I wasn't scared, and I didn't write down my thoughts. I just slept and watched television. I didn't have much of an appetite, and I didn't spend time with anyone outside of my family. I blocked out the world, my thoughts, and, most of all, my future.

When President Troutt called me from Rhodes and told me that he'd gotten me a spot as a St. Jude patient, I wondered why I hadn't even thought of St. Jude as an option. I think I had always associated St. Jude with small children, and I was nineteen years old. I also knew that Memphis was four hours away from home, and New Orleans was only two. I wanted to be at home for as much of my treatment as possible. Nonetheless, President Troutt talked to my mother about it, and we were both glad to get a second opinion. After researching Dr. Alberto Pappo online, I spoke with him on the phone. A renowned oncologist, he worked in the solid tumor clinic at St. Jude and handled many of the Ewing's sarcoma cases. I knew that I liked him immediately. From Mexico, he had a thick Hispanic accent, and it seemed he'd anticipated my call. Before I hung up the phone, he told me he would see me the next Monday. I guess I didn't have to make a decision after all. Dr. Pappo had made it for me. I checked into St. Jude Children's Research Hospital as a patient on May 24, 2010.

3

This Place is St. Jude

Before diagnosis, although I was excited to have been awarded the summer research internship, I knew very little about St. Jude Children's Research Hospital. I knew it was a place for children with cancer and other life-threatening illnesses. I knew it helped some people pay for their cancer treatment. I knew it did lots of breakthrough cancer research. Beyond these facts and the things I saw in fund raising ads, I knew almost nothing. But I loved chemistry, and being chosen for the internship made me feel honored and brilliant and inspired. I was going to have a chance to work in a laboratory and see if research was something I wanted to incorporate into my medical career. I, Margaret Carlisle Cupit, had been chosen to work on cancer research with one of the scientists at this internationally acclaimed hospital. This was exciting.

When I found out that I had cancer, though, my perfect plan was ruined. In some ways, I felt as though my entire life was ruined. I wondered whether cancer treatment would turn me off to hospitals and to cancer research and treatment. I wondered if it would turn me off to medicine entirely. What I didn't anticipate was that it would do just the opposite. During my summer at St. Jude I was able to experience the hospital not as a research helper but as a patient, and that gave me knowledge of and a passion for St. Jude that were far deeper than I could possibly have received otherwise. I also had the opportunity to help ALSAC (American Lebanese Syrian Associated Charities) promote St. Jude and raise funds to pay for the work St. Jude does, both treatment and research.

My first expectation about St. Jude was that it would be a very sad place. Cancer is sad enough as it is—the sickening treatment, the bald people, the hopelessness of their circumstances. Children's cancer, I thought, would be much sadder. Children are innocent, pure, happy, and carefree. They haven't experienced the world yet. They don't judge or hate. They are the last people you'd expect to get cancer. As I thought about bald, sick, and sometimes dying children, I imagined St. Jude as the saddest place on earth.

Try to picture what it must have felt like, to be so sick during the point in your life that you thought was going to be the best, not the worst. And everywhere around you, there are children—babies even—with the same awful disease taking the same awful medications that kill part of them in an attempt to save the rest. But in spite of this, every single employee you meet, whether it's the lady in the cafeteria or the nurse giving you your chemo or your own doctor, is an endless source of hope, light, and strength. This place is St. Jude.

The St. Jude mission is to extend life, yes, but it is more than that. The St. Jude mission is to make each moment in life as full of light and joy and hope and understanding and peace as possible. This goal applies to all patients, whether their prognosis is promising or extremely grave. This philosophy is so contagious that it's impossible not to adopt it for your own life, and because of it, St. Jude becomes completely different from anywhere else in the world. It becomes a place with no barriers of race or social class or language, a place where people of different religions pray together because they realize all are equally in need of a God who listens and of a place where money no longer means anything and where love and family mean everything.

When you walk into the revolving doorway, which serves also as an air purifier, you walk into a place different and apart from the rest of the world. The walls are not white or drab like most hospital walls. Instead, murals are painted around every corner. You look around, and you see pigs, squirrels, monkeys and bananas, forests, the four seasons, Mickey Mouse, and people of every color of the rainbow staring at you from the walls. There is not an empty wall in the place. Hanging in every hall are paintings done by St. Jude patients of every age and diagnosis. Large, comfortable couches occupy the front lobby, welcoming patients, family members, and visitors needing a rest or a break. Those couches would become a napping place for me on particularly long days.

Behind the security desk near the front of the hospital sit, not grumpy security guards, but friendly and engaging people. A gift store full of candy sits across the hall. Each clinic waiting room is a playroom, complete with arts and crafts, toys, a pretend kitchen, and children's books. There are child-life specialists and volunteers waiting to play with the children. Even the cafeteria exceeds the imagination, with foods from every part of the world and organic fruits and vegetables, often locally grown. The head chef was trained with a select group of other five-star chefs from around the country. Employees and patients actually enjoy eating in the St. Jude cafeteria. There are always activities going on right outside of the cafeteria: entertainment by musicians, clowns, and the like, and instruction in arts and crafts, such as knitting and guitar lessons. And there is a steady stream of celebrities visiting St. Jude to entertain the children.

Each St. Jude employee I encountered—from researcher to therapist, from social worker to cafeteria worker, from janitor to nurse, from doctor to radiologist—wants to be there, for he or she has dedicated his or her life to St. Jude's mission: finding cures and saving children. This is evident as you meet the people who work there, for all wear smiles and show compassion in every task they perform. Whether they are changing your sheets on the inpatient floor or serving you lunch, teaching you to walk again or listening to your heartbeat, St. Jude employees make the love for what they do apparent. They are the reason for the excellence of their hospital.

As if the brilliance and dedication of the people who staff St. Jude were not enough, we quickly realized that St. Jude was completely free. We had heard this before, and we thought that it was only the case for families without health insurance or in poverty. We were wrong, though. St. Jude accepted our insurance, but nothing else. This was made clear to us the first time we went to the pharmacy to pick up some medicine. My mom held her credit card out to the pharmacist, and the lady just laughed and said, "You must be new here. No, Ma'am, we don't take payment. "

Even if we tried to pay, St. Jude wouldn't let us. It was all free, for everyone. It took the financial stress off parents. It gave everyone one less thing to worry about during a time full of worries. Even our housing was free. Target House gave us a nice furnished apartment right down the road from the hospital at no charge at all and a gift card to Kroger every week for groceries. The financial burdens of cancer treatment can be tremendous.

Chemotherapy and all of the drugs that are used with it cost hundreds of thousands of dollars. Many families that have to pay for all of their medical expenses go into debt and file bankruptcy. I was once given an estimate that all of my treatment that year cost over two million dollars, but because of St. Jude, we didn't have to be consumed by anxiety over money.

Patients and their families come to St. Jude from all over the world. Every country, every culture, every race, every religion, every language, and every background is represented at St. Jude. Diversity takes on a whole new meaning. Perhaps the most amazing aspect of St. Jude, however, is not the diversity of the people, but the way in which these people get along. All of the barriers of class, socioeconomic status, race, religion, and language no longer matter within the walls of St. Jude, for there, all are united by a common goal: fighting cancer. With this in common, patients and patient families have the ability to connect quickly and to understand one another in ways that no one else can. They begin to lean on each other, bond with each other, and love each other. They become a family.

With my friends busy at college and unable to be around me much of the time because of my immune system, I began to spend a good bit of time with other St. Jude patients. Whether we attended dinners donated by the community at Target House or watched "The Bachelor" together on Monday nights (this part was my idea and sometimes required much encouragement), we enjoyed one another's company and the understanding that we offered each other. We distracted each other from the harshness of cancer treatment and appreciated each other for important reasons—not for how much money our families had, for what we looked like, or for what we were good at. We shared something that no one else could share with us; we were the only ones who understood what it was like to have cancer at this time in our lives.

I remember one especially bad day when I was sitting outside Target House. I had only one chemo left, but I felt terrible. Nothing seemed to be going right, and my counts were taking forever to recover. I'd been waiting for my last treatment for about five weeks, and my hair was starting to come back because I'd had such a long time without chemo. I was counting down the days and fed up with waiting.

One of my good friends at St. Jude was leaving. He had osteosarcoma, and he had finished his treatment and was doing really well. I was sad that he was leaving because he was from another country. He was one of those people who was always smiling, always brightening the room and my mood. He sat down beside me and, in his strong accent, asked me what was wrong.

I told him how frustrated I was with everything and how tired of waiting I was. He understood, he said. He had been there too. He told me not to lose faith in God, not to give up, and not to let myself have a bad attitude. He told me how lucky and blessed we were, and I knew he was right. Then he promised me that he was going to come to visit me every day in my last chemo, which lasted for five days. I told him that I would love that, but I really didn't think he'd actually show up.

I didn't find out that he really did come until after my last chemo was over, because I didn't remember that last treatment at all. My mom told me that he'd showed up every day and visited for a while, that he'd kept his promise and had helped get my mind off of the chemo. He was a good friend, a true friend, a friend I'll have forever. Our bond ran deep, even though we hadn't known each other very long. But that's how St. Jude relationships were. That's how they are.

When I first arrived at St. Jude, my sisters stayed at home with my grandmother Anne, while my parents and I moved to the Grizzly House. Grizzly house is a sort of hotel for St. Jude patients and family and is sponsored by the Memphis Grizzlies, a professional basketball team. We packed lightly after being told that we would be there for about a week. I was sure that I would be traveling back and forth between Memphis and Brookhaven for the treatments and that the first treatment would occur within the first week of my St. Jude stay. I was wrong about that and many other things. One thing about cancer and its treatment: they're unpredictable.

My first week at St. Jude was filled with every type of scan or test I could imagine. I had MRIs, CT scans, X-Rays, blood tests, urine tests, blood pressure tests, EKGs, and a bone marrow biopsy to make sure that my cancer hadn't spread to my bone marrow. I also had a wide spectrum of consultations: physical therapy, psychology, nutrition, social work, child life, and of course, appointments with my doctor, nurse practitioner, and nurse. From 8:00 a.m. to at least 3:00 p.m., my family and I would go from one appointment to the next, eating most of our meals in the hospital cafeteria. If we were finished early enough, we would go out to dinner in Memphis.

I don't remember crying much that first week. In fact, I don't remember crying at all. I know that I felt tired. My leg was still hurting from the biopsy, and I was still feeling pain from the tumor. My first chemo was quickly approaching, and my mom and I had heard that cutting my hair shorter would help me adjust to losing my hair more gradually. I decided that I would try it, that I might as well have short hair to see what it looked like. Four of my best friends from college drove to Memphis to see me that night. Sheerin, Macie, Arden, and Katherine were all there, crammed into our Grizzly House room, showing their love and support. They had with them a pair of purple hair-cutting scissors. I will never forget that night, the night we crowded into the tiny hotel bathroom in the worst of circumstances and had the best of times. For some reason, Arden was convinced that she knew how to cut hair. And for some reason, I trusted her. What did I have to lose? We stared into the mirror, joking and laughing, until someone suggested that we wet my hair. I sat down on the floor and leaned my head back into the bathtub as Macie helped me rinse my hair. Then we moved back to the mirror, and my friends gathered my wet brown hair and put it in a low ponytail. My stepfather Paul entered the room and told us to be quiet. He said something like, "There are sick people here!"

We quietly giggled and continued to talk and laugh. Arden cut off my ponytail and held it up for all of us to see. It was hilarious. After trimming a few uneven ends, we blow-dried my hair. It was surprisingly cute.

Most hospitals that treat pediatric cancer have one or two sections devoted to cancer treatment. St. Jude though, is different from most hospitals in this way, among many other ways. St. Jude divides cancer treatment into several clinics. A Clinic treats primarily leukemia and lymphomas. B Clinic is bone marrow transplant. D Clinic is the solid tumor clinic, and E Clinic is the brain tumor clinic. There is also C Clinic, for different specialties like limb sparing and wound care, and H Clinic for hematology. Since Ewing's sarcoma is a solid tumor, located in either bone or soft tissue like muscle, and since in my case the tumor was in my tibia and knee and in the muscle around these bones, I was treated in D clinic.

St. Jude also houses a variety of other services in different places in the hospital, such as Echo/EKG, surgery, procedures, dentistry, the medicine room (an ER of sorts), physical and occupational therapy, psychology, and social work, among others. In this way, St. Jude involves multiple healthcare professionals in the care of each patient and patient family, embodying the "team approach" to medicine.

There are many different doctors, nurse practitioners, and nurses within each specialty clinic. I had the honor of being primarily treated by my oncologist Dr. Alberto Pappo, my nurse practitioner Patti Peas, and my nurse Julie Morganelli. I also worked closely with Dr. Beth Stewart, a St. Jude physician fellow, and Christina, a physical therapy fellow.

I've heard stories before of people hating their oncologists because they associate them with the cancer and, in some ways, blame it on them. I have no such story to tell you. My "team," as I sometimes refer to them, was comprised of loving and caring (not to mention brilliant) individuals. I would never have been able to get through my cancer without them. They became not just medical caretakers, but important and inspiring friends and family.

Dr. Pappo is the very opposite of what I expected to find in an oncologist. Instead of serious, he was humorous. Instead of cynical, he was optimistic. Instead of building walls between himself and his patients, he built relationships with us. My clinic visits were usually a couple of times a week, scheduled after a visit to triage to get my blood counts checked and vital signs recorded. When I walked into the room, though, my blood counts were not the first thing Dr. Pappo addressed. He always asked me if I had seen any good movies lately, preferably funny ones. His recommendation for me when my spirits were low was always a trip to the movie theatre and a large bucket of popcorn mixed with chocolate candy. If I told him I had gained weight, which was a positive thing that I often viewed as a negative thing, he would simply reply, "Me too," while patting his stomach.

Having grown up in Mexico, Dr. Pappo speaks extremely quickly and with a strong accent. He also has a tendency to talk on and on about his adopted dogs, Mollie, Annie, and Bonnie, whom he loves like his family. He would sit on a rolling stool in the examining room and roll back and forth most of the time, unable to keep still. Usually, he would roll past the electric sink and paper towel dispenser, and the water and paper towels would go everywhere. This never ceased to startle him, and he never ceased to make us laugh.

Let me not overlook Dr. Pappo's intelligence. Before seeing him as my doctor I had searched his name online, and I knew that he was a world-renowned oncologist and researcher and had published many articles on childhood cancer. I had been placed under his care for a reason; he was the best. But Dr. Pappo was much more than an impressive resume and brilliant man. He was more than a physician or scientist. He did more than prescribe my medicines. He treated all of me, my entire being, my whole person. Because I took my medicine, washed my hands often, and did all the things I was supposed to do to stay healthy, he was able to focus on treating my spirit. So many times I walked into the clinic feeling sick and weak and frustrated and let down, and so many times I walked out of the clinic feeling uplifted and lucky and loved.

Dr. Pappo inspired his patients to beat cancer. Most of the time, his patients were survivors, but when they weren't, they still hadn't lost. My doctor cherished the people in his life and encouraged his patients to cherish the people in theirs, to live their lives to the fullest, and to laugh as much as possible. He always ended our visits with a hug and a kiss on the cheek as well as a simple, "I love you." I believe that the greatest doctors have the ability to do this, to allow themselves to bond with their patients, even the patients whom they know will likely not survive.

But I also learned from my year in treatment that a physician does not stand alone. He or she needs a team, and each member of my team was just as valuable as the next. The mastermind behind organizing and putting into place the decisions that Dr. Pappo made about my treatment, including filling my prescriptions and getting all the details about my many side effects in order to mitigate them, was Patti.

When I think of Patti, I think of comfort. I picture a tall, lean, perfectly poised and oh-so-elegant woman, taking notes on the back of whatever piece of paper was handy—often a folded paper towel or printout of my lab results. Complimented by genuine inner beauty and a sense of peace, Patti's beauty radiates into the whole room. Patti devoted ample amounts of time to me every time I was in the clinic and returned my calls quickly when I left her messages—even in the years following my treatment. Patti was careful, thorough, and precise. If I had a problem, she always found an answer, and she was so skilled at what she did that she could look at me and, based on my appearance, tell me whether or not I needed a blood transfusion. Patti and I also shared a lot of laughs, since we have the same sense of humor and set of inside jokes. She always found a way to make me realize there were things worth living for.

And then there was Julie. Sweet and Southern, with a thick accent and the ability to talk with enthusiasm about anything and everything, Julie was the perfect nurse for me. She was a great storyteller, with an animated face that lit up every room she entered. Despite her vivacious persona, I trusted Julie with a needle more than any nurse in the whole hospital. Whether she was accessing my port or trying to put an IV in one of my chemo-damaged veins, Julie never missed.

Julie's emotional depth should not be overlooked, however. The first time one of the patients I had met passed away, I went to Julie, knowing that she had lost many patients during her time at St. Jude and would understand. She told me that her profession was one where doing her best was always enough, and that the patients who survived—like me—made it worth the heartache.

This view was also held by Beth, a pediatrician doing her fellowship at St. Jude and on her way to becoming a licensed pediatric oncologist. Since she spent a lot of time working in the solid tumor clinic and with Dr. Pappo, Beth and I often crossed paths. At some point, though, Beth became much more than an employee we talked to while we were at the hospital and a doctor we asked for advice. She became one of my best friends. We even traveled together to speak on behalf of St. Jude at a Delta Delta Delta conference in Dallas (the Tri-Delta sorority has St. Jude as a national charity).

Beth was in her late twenties, and I was almost twenty, so we weren't that far apart in age. Beyond that, though, she didn't act as old as the other doctors did. She made an effort to relate to me, so I felt like I could talk to her about boys and college and all of my feelings. I also admired her. She was brilliant, kind, grounded, self-aware, and successful—not to mention beautiful. Somehow, she has remained humble despite all of these qualities. She was everything I wanted to be one day.

Perhaps what most drew me to Beth was that she treated me as her equal. She listened to me as closely as I listened to her. When she asked me how I was feeling, she did it in a way that showed she cared. She waited for my answers, even when she already knew how badly I was feeling. Whether I was in the hospital for fever or an infection or chemo, Beth always stopped by. She would sit on my bed with me and get my mind off of my situation. She would entertain me when there was nothing to do. She made me feel appreciated, loved, and fun to spend time with. She was also funny, had great stories to tell, and could answer all of my medical questions. When Beth was around, I found myself enjoying the days I was inpatient. Once, when I was stuck in the hospital the week of Christmas, she even brought Christmas decorations for my room. We were more than patient and doctor; we were friends. Beth was the type of doctor who would do anything for her patients, completely devoted and dedicated to them beyond the call of duty. Beth is still one of my most treasured friends, and I have come to see her as a part of my family. If I can be the half the doctor she is one day, I will have reached my goal. Who knows, maybe one day we will even be St. Jude doctors together.

At the beginning of my second week at St. Jude, Dr. Pappo went over the incredibly long list of side effects for each of the chemotherapy drugs I would be receiving. Most people know that chemo causes nausea and vomiting as well as fatigue, and some people know that it also causes mouth sores and diarrhea, but few people know about the other side effects that chemo can cause. Dr. Pappo told me that there were four side effects I would get, without a doubt: nausea, vomiting, hair loss, and neutropenia (neutropenia is when the body has a below normal amount of neutrophils, the type of white blood cells that fight disease). The list of rare side effects went on and on. It included heart problems, kidney problems, liver problems, bone problems, seizures, stroke, anemia, infection, swelling and fluid retention, infertility, rashes, numbness, allergic reactions, destruction of mucous membranes in the digestive tract (all the way from the mouth to the anus), nerve problems, bleeding or bruising, depletion of platelets, depression or anxiety, and in rare cases, death. It would be an understatement to say that this list made me nervous.

After I knew all of the possible things that could go wrong in chemo, I wasn't quite as confident going into treatment. However, I was still determined to get through it with few difficulties. I thought I was tougher than a lot of people and that chemo wouldn't make me sick if I didn't let it. To tell the truth, the first chemo really wasn't that bad. I was given lots of anti-nausea drugs, including Benadryl and Ativan as well as Dexamethasone, a steroid used as an anti-inflammatory. All of the drugs made me sleep for most of the time, and though I didn't feel very hungry, I didn't feel all that sick, either.

On one of the last days of that first five-day chemo treatment, my mom was out of the room when I got out of bed to use the restroom. I dragged my IV pole behind me. As I walked out of the bathroom, I began to vomit. It wasn't like the stomach virus. It was much more violent and gut wrenching. I felt like I couldn't stop, and my mouth tasted like metal and bile and acid. I sank to the ground and felt like I was going to faint. The room started to get dark. A nurse ran to me with a wet washcloth and pressed it to my forehead. I began to cry for my mama, and someone ran to get her. I climbed back into bed, but I didn't stop crying, even when Mama got there. I realized then that chemo wasn't what I thought. It wasn't going to be easy. Little did I know, it would get much, much worse.

I wish I could write a detailed description of every chemotherapy treatment, but I can't. Perhaps this is actually not a bad thing. The nausea was so constant and terrible that I was given the maximum doses of every anti-nausea drug available to me. As a result, I wasn't myself during chemo, and, as a result, I do not remember much of it. What I do remember comes to me at random in quick, vivid images. I often wonder why I can remember certain moments while others are gone as quickly as they came. My "chemo memories" are a lot like dreams. They are very difficult to describe, often quite foggy, and come and go, despite my wishes.

My first chemotherapy treatment was just a tiny preview of what chemo would be like for me. I quickly learned that if I was not asleep during chemo then I was sick, and by sick I mean constantly vomiting. Upon beginning each treatment, I would get into my hospital room and change into my pajamas. I would stay in these pajamas for days at a time, because changing clothes required me to get out of bed, and that was something I couldn't do during chemo. I couldn't leave the bed because any movement at all made me more nauseous and more miserable. For the same reason, I couldn't get out of bed and drag my IV pole across the room to the restroom. Having crutches and a hurt leg made this even more complicated. So I was introduced to the bedside toilet, a lovely plastic toilet that reminded me of a training toilet and sat right next to my bed.

Not only did I have to use the restroom in a small toilet right next to my bed without any privacy, but I also had to use the restroom a lot. Chemotherapy is extremely bad for the kidneys (extremely bad for everything, really), so I was hooked up to IV fluids that ran at a very fast rate in order to get the chemo into and out of my body as quickly as possible. Every two hours, I was required to empty my bladder, so every two hours I had to wake up and get out of bed. This usually meant that every two hours, I would start dry heaving again.

There was always a taste in my mouth, too—very distinctive yet impossible to describe. I would lie there, up to six days at a time, tasting the vomit in my mouth. Yes, I believe it was vomit that I tasted, or perhaps a mixture of vomit and every medicine I ever had to take in my lifetime. Maybe it was the IV fluids I could taste. I was connected to giant bags of IV fluids, usually just sodium ions and a bunch of water, but sometimes even dextrose to help me put on weight. The bags were connected to my port, so I could constantly feel the bubbly liquid oozing into my body. It gave me heartburn and a weird, scratchy feeling in my stomach. During chemo, I wouldn't eat at all. I knew that eating would only lead to more vomiting. But despite my constant nausea, I was incredibly hungry at all times. I would fall asleep as more Benadryl was pushed into my system, thinking about the pizza and pasta and donuts that I couldn't possibly keep down but wanted so very badly.

I do remember that on chemo number three, famous country music stars Naomi and Wynona Judd came to visit me in the hospital. Naomi held my hand and told me about her experience with chemotherapy when she had hepatitis. We exchanged mailing addresses and she later mailed me a necklace of hers that was engraved with the word "hope." I am still amazed that my experience connected me to Naomi and that she could understand me on a deep level because she knew what I was going through. Chemo number three was also the treatment when I began hating Pop-Tarts. I quickly learned that eating things in chemo led to hating them for at least a couple of years afterwards.

After each chemotherapy treatment, I would leave the hospital attached to a large bag of IV fluids. My mother would push me in my wheelchair because I was far too weak to walk. I was really too weak even to stand up. I remember the routine after chemo. We would usually leave the hospital late at night because it took the pharmacy a while to get my fluids. We were allowed to stay an extra night inpatient but that was the last thing I wanted to do. Staying in the hospital made me sicker than I would be if I left.

When we had gathered all of our things and all of my medicines and IV fluids, we would drive back to Target House. On the way back, though, we often stopped at McDonald's because I was starving and it was the only place on the road back to Target House that was open that late. I know it seems strange—the nausea instantly disappearing when I left the hospital—but that's how it was for me. Keep in mind that I didn't eat at all during chemo, so I was ravenous after five days with no food. I would usually get a large order of french fries, eat all of them with generous amounts of dipping sauce, and spill honey mustard on myself due to the drugs that hadn't worn off yet. This was one of the few times in my life that I can remember eating a large order of McDonald's french fries without feeling a bit guilty.

After we got back to our apartment, I would go straight to the tub. I felt the need to be clean after several days without a bath or shower and especially after having that nasty tasting and smelling chemo pumped through my body. Mama would help me undress and climb into the tub, carefully keeping my IV fluids and tubing as well as my port out of the water. I could barely stand on my own, and several times I nearly collapsed. I was the definition of weak.

After my bath, Mama would help me to my bed, and I would happily settle in. For the next few days, all I wanted was sleep and lots of water. The nausea was mostly gone at that point, but then the pain began. My entire body ached. I felt like I had been run over by an eighteen-wheeler. I felt bruised and sore and achy all over. It hurt to move, to roll over in bed, to touch my arm or leg. Everything hurt. I often described it as feeling like my whole body had been bruised. Everything I touched hurt. I wasn't allowed to take Advil or Tylenol because they could mask a fever. Because fever can be dangerous when a person's counts are low, it is important to monitor it throughout the time of treatment. Also, because I had a port, there was always the risk that I could become septic very quickly if I had an infection in my body. Instead of Advil or Tylenol, I had to take the strong pain medicine that had been prescribed for my leg.

Those first few days out of chemo, I would also start feeling a strange sensation in my throat. I would tell my mom that it felt like there were "cats and dogs fighting in my throat" or "ants crawling through my digestive tract." I felt the need to tell what couldn't be told in words. I sometimes had the sensation from my mouth all the way through my digestive tract. There was no way to be comfortable, except during sleep.

Before surgery, I received chemo every couple of weeks. My blood counts—white blood cells, red blood cells, and platelets—recovered very quickly. Sometimes I had to get blood or platelet transfusions for an extra boost; thankfully they always seemed to help. After my surgery, though, my counts didn't recover on time for my next scheduled chemo. My nurse practitioner Patti, would say that my bone marrow was "tired" or "worn out." This was, perhaps, the most frustrating part of going through chemotherapy. When my body wasn't ready for chemo, we had no choice but to wait until it was ready. If you were wondering what would have happened if we did chemo anyway, then the answer is that I would have gotten very, very sick. People can't survive without platelets or enough red and white blood cells. All I could do was wait.

You may be wondering how I survived if I couldn't eat during chemo. Patti told me that I had to "play catch up;" between chemo sessions I had to gain back the weight I had lost. There were days when this was deeply upsetting to me. One of the most wonderful things about Patti was that she refused to dismiss any of my emotional problems as irrelevant or unimportant. In the midst of the fight for my life, concern with my former obsession with weight would appear. Patti understood this concern, being a perfectionistic young woman herself. The most helpful thing she ever said to me regarding my weight was that focusing too much on weight had caused her to miss out on all the other wonderful things in her life. Even though I was going through chemo, there were wonderful things to be noticed, and obsession with my weight was not going to help me see them. I began turning away from the scale during appointments, looking away from the number.

For a while, allowing myself to indulge in any and every type of food I desired was a sufficient way for me to maintain my weight. Eventually, though, near the end of chemo, my appetite grew tired as my body grew tired, and my doctor was forced to threaten me with a feeding tube. If this doesn't sound bad already, then let me explain to you that it was a nasal-gastric feeding tube, the kind that goes through the nose and into the stomach. Needless to say, I was determined not to get a feeding tube. One day I was told that I had to gain weight by my next clinic appointment, which was a few days later. That day, I went back to the apartment and sat down on the couch with a jar of peanut butter. I literally ate the entire jar as a snack. I also had several other big meals and deserts that day. When I returned for my appointment two days later, I had gained four pounds. I did not have to get the feeding tube after all, thanks to my love for peanut butter.

Besides the amount of peanut butter I ate, one of the only other things I had control over was my physical rehabilitation. Having cancer and going through cancer treatment took away almost all of my control. I had no control over how I felt, what I looked like, or what I did with my time. I had no control over the pace of my treatment, how quickly it went, or when I would get home. I couldn't decide when I got to be in public places, when I could allow my friends to visit, or when I had to stay for hours at the hospital to get blood and platelet transfusions. By the time my surgery came around, I had been refraining for several months from putting any weight on my right leg. Then, after surgery, in addition to atrophied muscles, I had a titanium rod for a tibia and a titanium artificial knee. Only one third of the way through my chemotherapy treatments, it was time for me to learn to use my leg again. Not only was I expected to do my leg exercises at physical therapy; I was also expected to do the exercises between physical therapy sessions. For the first time in the process of fighting cancer, I had a choice to make. My choice, of course, was to take action, but much of this motivation came from an external source—Christina.

Christina was a fellow at St. Jude. She was finishing her training for pediatric physical therapy, so she was only there for several months. During those months, she and I bonded at a deep level, and she became my good friend. After the first six weeks after surgery, I was allowed to bend my leg again. I expected to bend it normally, but I was shocked when I found that impossible. I would lie on my stomach, and Christina would stretch out my knee by pushing my leg farther and farther into a bend. It was extremely painful at times, and I often squeezed a toy football in an attempt not to cry.

In the months following surgery, I spent hours each week in physical therapy, rebuilding my leg muscles and learning to walk again. The physical therapy was grueling, painful, and exhausting. After every chemo, I would drag myself into PT and fight nausea and fatigue. Needless to say, I would take a few steps forward between treatments and take a few steps back right after treatments. Because of chemo, my wound kept getting infected, refusing to heal properly. This made physical therapy even more difficult. But I kept forcing myself to work harder and did my leg exercises almost every day.

While Christina worked with me, she talked to me about her life. And she listened to me. In fact, she was an amazing listener. And every time I felt discouraged about something in physical therapy, whether it was that my leg wasn't bending as much as I wanted it to or that I was just too tired or discouraged to keep going, she hugged me and listened to me cry. She helped me through the hardest parts of my days. When I woke up in the morning, I looked forward to the hour I would get to spend with her in physical therapy, an hour with a good friend.

I remember how I felt when I took my first steps without crutches. Of course, I was wobbly and barely making it on my own, but I was walking on two legs without holding onto anything at all. I started crying, overwhelmed with pride and gratitude. I knew that I had worked hard to get to that point, but I also knew that Christina had worked equally hard to get me there. Although I was sad when she finished her fellowship and left St. Jude at the end of the semester, I looked forward to dancing at her wedding.

St. Jude taught me that happiness had to be found and seized in the little things. Whether it was in a large order of McDonald's french fries, in laughing at Dr. Pappo's jokes, in asking Christina questions about her fiancé, or in Mama's tucking me in at night, it was still happiness. Because of

St. Jude and the people who shaped my experience there, my year of cancer treatment not only had its downside, it also had lots of upside.

When it came time to leave, I had gained a lot of things. I had gained courage, strength, hope, inspiration, optimism, understanding, and faith. I had gained countless new role models and many dear friends. Some of these friends I got to see recover, and a few I had to see leave this world behind. They did it with grace and strength. I gained a life goal and a new passion for life. But I think the most important thing I walked away with was an overwhelming understanding of life and a sense of gratitude for it.

4

Of Squirrels and Theology

EHH

In the first month of what turned into an eleven-month treatment ordeal, Maggie received tons of messages, even from persons who did not know her, promising prayers and assuring her that all would be well. Maggie, of course, was trying to make sense of what was happening to her, not just for the sake of understanding but to know how to live, perhaps even how to die.

Some who sent words of encouragement were also searching. What does one say? Does it really mean anything to say "you're going to be fine" or "God has a plan for you" or "There is a reason for everything?" Such words may be well intended, yet who can explain how all will work out or believe that the "plan" of a loving God might include giving one cancer?

On the other hand, if one is the patient's mother, father, sister, step-parent, close friend or grandparent, comforting words are not enough. One is also trying to make sense of the thing that has happened. For it has happened not only to the patient; it has happened to oneself. So it was for Nini and me. We wanted to help, and there wasn't much we could do but speak words that would encourage and help ease the pain and fear brought on by this dreadful event. It was as though the words we sent to Maggie were part of our own process of coming to terms with this ongoing collision with the hard rocks of reality. We would, of course, go to visit and so be present both to Maggie and to her mother Ellie. But what could we do until Maggie and Ellie were ready to receive us and we were able to make the drive to Memphis?

We could live and respond out of our own faith. We could pray. We could ask our church community and our friends to pray. We could speak or write such words of love and wisdom as we were given, letting expressions of faith strengthen us even as we offered them to Maggie and Ellie.

Nini is especially good at talking with the suffering and the dying. She has an inspired gift for speaking directly, honestly, and compassionately to them out of the resources of her faith. On the other hand, I have difficulty knowing what to say in situations of pain and uncertainty, and, even if I think I know what should be said, I lack courage for saying it. Forty-six years of teaching philosophy of religion and philosophical theology in the safe setting of the classroom may have enabled me to settle my mind about God and God's ways with the world, but a settled mind is not a settled heart. Besides, classroom lectures were not fitting in the circumstances. Nevertheless, knowing that Maggie is both smart and thoughtful, it seemed possible that a bit of philosophy and theology might at some point and in some way be a gift I could offer. In any case, Nini and I would send such words of love and encouragement as we could until we were able to visit her at St. Jude. But what could we say? What should we say?

Maggie helped us. She began writing a CaringBridge journal shortly after she was settled at Target House. The journal entries gave insight about her condition at the beginning of the torturous treatments—physical, intellectual, psychological, and spiritual— and this helped us know better what to say. Maggie continued the journal throughout the year at St. Jude, and it is in reading her entries that we witness faith taking shape in Maggie's life. The first several entries surprised us with their depth even as they exhibited the wonderful humor and exuberance of her personality.

MCC, SUNDAY, MAY 30, 2010

They told me it would probably hit me today, and I still haven't gotten sick at all! I can't believe that this is so easy so far. Either I am one of those really lucky people who don't get side effects, or I will start feeling bad in the near future. I'm not just lucky that I am not feeling badly, though. The past few weeks have taught me a lot. I think I have more faith. I don't know if it's faith in God or faith in my family or faith in friends or faith in the medical profession, but I know that faith is coming from somewhere. Sure, there are moments when I completely panic and forget how to breathe and want to scream at God and the world because I, of all people, have cancer. But then I remember what else I have: an attentive and supportive family and a group of friends that continue to amaze me. And, somehow, even though I am cooped up in a tiny hospital room all day and all night, I know that I am the luckiest person in the world.

MCC, FRIDAY, JUNE 4, 2010

Today I had my first tantrum since I was diagnosed, and I'm beginning to think that maybe it was overdue. I was talking to Mama and my grandmother Anne about how I need to be more careful about germs. You may know this, but I'll explain.

When you get chemotherapy, it kills all the quickly dividing cells in your body. That means it kills the cancer cells, but also things like red blood cells, hair, and white blood cells. Fewer or no white blood cells or a low ANC (absolute neutrophil count) means you have no immune system. Any germs can make you deathly ill. Because of this, soon I will not be able to have so many visitors—or any at all. When I do, we will all wear masks. No sick people or people who have been near sick people in the last week will be allowed to be near me. And when I do have visitors, they won't get to stay very long. Fifteen minutes is usually all I will get. Obviously, this is not what I want. No one wants to be a hermit (except hermits; no offense if you are one).

So I went in my little room in Target House and sat on my twin bed with the Disney princess comforter and cried. I wept. I screamed. I kicked. I sniffled. I yelled. I cried until I couldn't breathe, and then I cried more. I'm not saying this in a public forum because I want your sympathy. I just think it was really good for me to come a little closer to realizing that the cancer in my leg is real. It's as real as the blood that runs through my veins. And I didn't do anything to deserve this.

Life happens, and it doesn't stop happening, and it rarely slows down, but that's how it is. I'll never be able to turn back time and be normal again, and that is enough for anyone to be angry about, especially me. Sometimes my entire body hurts from chemo, and I wonder how many more days I can put up with this. But then there are moments, like when I put on the polka-dotted socks someone gave me today and when I sit down and read organic chemistry and when Mama tells the only joke she knows (which you should hear), there are moments when I forget about the cancer and remember that I am alive right now in this moment, that I am breathing and smiling and loving and feeling, and even if I feel some pain, I am okay. I am still Maggie. I will get through this year by savoring the moments that make life what it is: a gift.

MCC, TUESDAY, JUNE 8, 2010

I'm waiting for my second chemo treatment to start. I'm supposed to start Friday, but if my ANC is below 750 I'll have to wait longer. My body has to recover before we start wiping it out again. I am dreading it a little bit, mostly because I will be drugged and in a hospital bed and be woken up to take my temperature every few hours. But I'm not as scared as I was before the first treatment. Now I know what to expect. I think. I hope. I could be very wrong, because the drugs will be different this time.

Today, a random kid made my day. I was sitting in the clinic, waiting to speak to my nurse about something, and I sat down beside her. She stared at me, one of those very obvious stares, and I smiled back. I asked her what her name was (I can't remember it now), and I told her mine. I looked down at her wrist and noticed that she had a lot of silly bands, those little rubber bands shaped like animals and stuff that everybody likes for some strange reason. I told her they were cool. Her little sister soon joined us. Her arm was covered in the bracelets as well. And then, the little girl pulled off four of her bracelets and gave them to me. I don't know how much they cost or how many more she had at home. I don't know what kind of cancer she had or how good her prognosis was. All I know is that, for some reason, her giving me her bracelets made me really happy.

MCC, WEDNESDAY, JUNE 9, 2010

When you find out that you have cancer, you close your eyes a lot. You keep closing them, hoping that when you open them you will wake up from this long nightmare that you keep having about cancer. When I close my eyes, I see a hot, dry parking lot with a million shiny cars and a glare brighter than the sun itself. There is no water anywhere, and my mouth is drier than it is during chemo treatments; it also has an unbearable metallic vomit taste. I am smothering, bundled up in clothing that is too difficult to remove, and my face is covered with excess amounts of hot, sticky makeup. I am alone and annoyed and angry, but I am not allowed to show it. My throat aches with tears, and my eyes burn as if they have been sprayed with acid. The worst part of all is that there is absolutely nothing I can do about it; it is just how I feel. I want to feel rain, clouds, wind, and ice. I want to feel comforted and valuable. I want to be myself again, away from the glare and the heat. I need relief.

When I open my eyes, I see a white wall. I see the balloons that were given to me as well as the bulletin board my little sister made for me. I see a room where someone lives, not a hotel room or a temporary place of visit, but a permanent bedroom. And I realize that I am stuck here, too.

Here is a question I really haven't asked myself much: why is cancer scary? Why does it make me feel trapped? What, exactly, am I afraid of? I guess that's kind of like asking a little kid why they are afraid of the dark. The answer? There are so many possibilities. So much can happen in the dark. Bugs can crawl on you without your permission, you can fall and hurt yourself, robbers can hide in your closet unnoticed. So I guess the answer is the same with cancer. Cancer and the drugs that try to kill it can make you vomit, ache, sweat, burn, lose your immune system, lose your taste buds, lose your energy, get mouth sores, twitch. Trust me, you don't want me to list all the possible side effects they showed me.

Cancer can even kill you. I suppose that is the worst-case: dying. People are so afraid of dying. I think we have a natural instinctual drive to survive, to avoid death. And we fear death more than anything. I know a lot of people who hide that fear, who use their faith to deny it, or who just avoid it altogether. But none of us want to die. Maybe because, when we die, we have absolutely no control over what happens to us. Something else controls us. So it seems to me that my biggest fear is losing control by allowing something else to move me through the universe, or by simply allowing a drug to destroy parts of my body in an attempt to destroy my tumor.

I may be crazy, and I may be unlike all of you who read this, but it feels really good to take a deep breath and realize that we are not in control of anything, but something else is—something far wiser and far more intricate. And because I don't have to be in control, all I have to do is sit back and try to enjoy the ride.

MCC, WEDNESDAY, JUNE 16, 2010

I finished my second chemo treatment, and it was very bad. I'm sure no reader would like to read the details of today, of how this morning at 5:00 a.m. I started vomiting and couldn't stop until the late afternoon. So I will spare you for now. Because I am feeling a little bit better, and I'm kind of proud of that. I think that, at least to some extent, I willed my body to stop getting sick. I got to a point today when I was fed up with this whole process: the little hairs falling out on my pillow, having to drag around an IV fluid bag and pump, puking my guts out every time I moved. I told myself that I was going to feel better, that there was no way I could be this sick much longer. So I ate a bean burrito from Taco Bell and took a nap. I'm still okay, and it's been a couple of hours. If I could talk to my cancer, here is what I'd say:

> Dear Mr. Cancer,
> I don't approve of you trying to ruin my life.
> I don't approve of you pulling all of my hair out.
> I don't approve of you telling me what I can and cannot eat, who I can and cannot see, and that all of this happened for a reason.
> I don't approve of the pain you cause in my leg.
> I don't approve of the night sweats that you used to send.
> I don't approve of you telling me you would take my appetite and my joy, and that there is nothing I can do about it.
> So just because you picked my beautiful body to jump inside and screw around with does not mean that you've won. I have every reason to fight, and you have none. I feel sorry for you and your need to prey on healthy people, good people. But I refuse to allow you to ruin my life, my year, or even another day.
> Sincerely,
> Maggie Cupit
> P.S. Do not write back. (I do not care!)

MCC, SUNDAY, JUNE 20, 2010

I love squirrels. I'm still not sure why, but I know that our connection is undeniable. My grandmother Anne reported a few days ago that there was a place outside Target House with lots of friendly squirrels. She said that these squirrels ran up to her and sat at her feet, as if they were waiting for something. Then she saw lots of peanut shells, and she told us that the squirrels would eat the peanuts. I was very jealous, due to my obsession with squirrels. So today it was my mission to feed those squirrels.

But let's face it. Our missions rarely go as planned. At least that's the case for me. After putting on some clothes and my owl hat, as well as a mask because my counts are down (no immune system). I crutched myself to the elevator and out of Target House. I was in good spirits and my body was working correctly, so I was thankful. And then I stepped outside. I immediately felt like I was in one of those saunas where you're supposed to throw water on rocks and produce steam and lie on wooden boards without very much clothing and soak up the heat or something. It wasn't relaxing, though. Breathing into and from a mask is hot and stuffy, so the temperature increased at least ten degrees for me, personally. But there's also another problem. I'm going through menopause due to the medication that protects my ovaries from chemotherapy (or is supposed to and may or may not be effective), so I started having a hot flash or something like it while I was in the heat. Keep in mind that this is all in a span of several seconds. My heart started racing and I felt dizzy, so Mama pulled the car up so Anne and I could get in. The air conditioning helped a lot, but when we got to Kroger, I started feeling emotional. Now, I've always considered myself a very emotionally mature and observant individual. But this time, like a lot of times lately, I didn't know what was making me cry. I was just crying. There is a big chance that one of the seventy-four drugs I am currently taking causes me to be more emotional, but I wondered if there was more to it. Obviously, I am allowed to cry as much as I want and expected to sometimes because I have cancer and the only treatment involves destroying my body. But this time I thought about Paul Tillich.

Paul Tillich was a Christian existentialist philosopher, and my grandmother Anne recently bought one of his books and told my mother and me about him. I know nothing about him and have not studied his writing yet, so don't take any of this to heart. But from what I have gathered, Tillich believed in prayer and interpreted Paul's readings a little differently than most people do. Here is my flawed understanding:

God—or whatever it is that we language-oriented creatures assign the name of God to—is too complicated and vast and powerful for our human minds to begin to understand. So when we pray, using words that humans created, it isn't enough. I have often stayed up late thinking about the existence of God and wondering how, if God did exist, talking to him or her with my language would be effective at all. In some ways, this type of prayer isn't the truest form of prayer. The same goes for ritualistic prayers. And I sometimes wonder why we need prayer. If God is all-knowing or all-powerful, why should I spend my time telling something what it already knows or asking it for something it has already decided to give or deny me? But somehow, when we stop thinking and begging and thanking and nagging and just allow our minds to quiet a little, true prayer happens. The deepest senses of longing and joy and sadness and tiredness that we feel in these moments, perhaps these are prayers. That which we cannot describe with words, and which we often ruin when we do try, maybe that is prayer. The deepest things that we think and feel beyond the grasp of language and society, I think these things are prayers. And maybe our openness—open hearts and open minds and, if you're into yoga, open hands facing the ceiling as you lie on your back in corpse position—maybe our openness is the best way for us to pray. Because sometimes, in those moments, something happens, something I won't try to put in words, something bigger than the adjective "godly" can explain. And in those moments, He or She or It speaks to us, comforts us, or tells us what to pray for next.

Though ending my journal entry here would be the most poetic thing to do, I still haven't told you everything. After we went to Kroger, we came back to Target House with peanuts. And I took a two hour nap from 5:00 p.m. till 7:00 p.m. (I acknowledge how strange this naptime is). When I woke up, we went outside to see the squirrels. It was now much cooler, but there was one problem. There were no squirrels. We kept looking and looking and calling for them as if they were dogs, and nothing happened. I was fed up and angry at the squirrels for hiding from me. I began to wonder if Anne was going senile. But then Mama spotted a squirrel in a tree, sprawled out and napping. We went to the bottom of the tree and threw some peanuts on the ground. Minutes later, one, two, three squirrels trickled down the tree onto the ground and approached us. When I put peanuts inches from my feet, they would come and get them. We watched them eat and scamper and frolic as squirrels always do, and one of them started burying peanuts in nearby flower beds. It was the perfect end to my day. Then we came back to the room and made a two-layer Funfetti cake, complete with many sprinkles and a lot of icing. I can rest now.

OF SQUIRRELS AND THEOLOGY

EHH

These early journal entries helped Nini and me know what to say in communicating with Maggie before our first visit. They gave us a particular Maggie, a Maggie with intellectual and psychological depth and with a spiritual life of which she herself was perhaps only beginning to be aware. We were encouraged that in the very first journal entry she was speaking of faith. We responded quickly by email to encourage it: "You wonder what your faith is in. Is it in physicians and nurses, your family, your friends, yourself? Why not all of them? You have support from all over, more support than you could ever dream of. And it all matters." At this early point at the beginning of the treatment process, we were hopeful that things would continue along this path, which did not seem terribly difficult. We were also hopeful that Maggie would be able to sustain the sense of having faith. As the treatments became ever more challenging, she found herself living a life of faith she had not even dreamed about.

In her journal, we see Maggie oscillating from courage to fear, from the sense of being "the luckiest person in the world" to anger at having cancer and of having lost forever the "normal" life she had enjoyed before, from the sense of being burdened with responsibility for this part of her life to the sense of being free to "sit back and try to enjoy the ride." These emotions may well be typical of cancer patients, yet Maggie speaks wisely—and theologically—in expressing them.

"Life is a gift," she says. Death is scary because it is a complete loss of control. God is beyond human comprehension. We use words to address God but words are never adequate to the job. God cannot be simply masculine or feminine, so "He, She, It." Nevertheless, Maggie finds herself still speaking of God in personal terms: "something else is [in control]—something wiser and more intricate" and "He or She or It *speaks* to us, *comforts* us, or *tells* us what to pray for next."

The philosopher/theologian in me says "Yes!" Maggie knows that while God is not simply masculine or feminine, God is *at least* personal. For God acts intentionally and with intricate wisdom to comfort, speak, and exercise control. But there is much ambiguity in the idea of divine control or providence, and many of the messages from well-wishers were suggesting that God controls by causing evil and suffering as part of a grand plan to secure some unseen and mysterious good for the sufferer. If that were God's way, then God had caused Maggie to have cancer, which would ultimately somehow be good for her.

I do not believe that God causes cancer or accidental deaths in order to secure good, and I did not believe it would encourage Maggie to think that way. Here, then, was an important question to address. Talking about it with Nini, we decided that some words from Tolkien's *Lord of the Rings* might be helpful.

Early in *The Fellowship of the Ring*, Frodo laments that he was born in the time when the evil Sauron is regaining power and that the terrible Ring of Power had now become his responsibility. Gandalf wisely instructs Frodo that we do not get to choose the time and circumstances of our lives. "All we have to decide," says Gandalf, "is what to do with the time that is given us."[1]

We hoped Gandalf's words would suggest a healthy way to think about God's ways with the world and would encourage Maggie to think not about what caused her cancer but about what to do with the life and time given her. Tolkien's perspective makes it clear that providence is everywhere at work, but he does not present the work of providence as an external cause forcing events against the nature of things and against the character of persons. Rather, Tolkien's story shows God's providential action as hidden in the ordinary operations of things and the characteristic actions of persons. It may be possible for those who are attuned to God's active role in the world to sense providential events as they unfold. So Gandalf senses that a power other than Sauron was at work in Bilbo's finding the Ring, and so Elrond recognizes that the burden of carrying the Ring in the quest for its destruction was a burden "appointed" for Frodo. Nevertheless, it is only after the fact that persons can recognize events as providential, can see what has in fact been done by God. Furthermore, in Tolkien's story, God does not cause evil things to happen in order to secure good. Nevertheless, God acts, in spite of the randomness of nature and the finitude and wickedness of persons, to secure divine good for those who will receive it—and this even if the evils out of which good is brought include the evils of cancer and early death. Tolkien's words would undoubtedly need some explanation, but we thought they might be helpful as a start.

Another point of contact was in Maggie's wonderful squirrel entry, in which in addition to her delightful account of seeking out and feeding the squirrels, she cites Paul Tillich and offers an understanding of prayer

1. Tolkien, *The Fellowship of the Ring*, 50.

that both reveals her questioning mind and her openness to God. Here was a nineteen-year-old who seemed already to know that the truest form of prayer is not telling God what to think and what to do, but bringing ourselves before God in silence to receive what God has for us: God's wisdom, God's forgiveness, God's delight in us, God's love for us, God's transformative action in our souls.

So we sent emails ahead of our first visit.

Nini, Monday, June 21, 2010

Dear One,

We love reading your thoughts—so deep and honest. I especially loved your musings on prayer. In the beginning was the Word and the Word was with God and the Word was God; we know that. We start prayer with words; in the beginning it is a grocery list of what we expect from God. As we mature on the journey, we realize what you have, that God already knows. Sometimes, though, it is wonderful to hear ourselves say what we are asking because we see where we really are in joy, or pain, or confusion. But when the journey gets deeper, we come to know that quietness where He, She, It *is* and where words are not necessary. Suddenly we see it is not about us. It is about Him, Her It, and sitting quietly allows that voice to be heard within us, and it gives joy, strength, love, and comfort but also regret, confession, and awareness of failure. Once you hear that Voice, there is no denying that it is real. You are right; too much attention is sometimes given to the memorized prayer or the correct format. But those forms do help serve as a way of learning and they can become mantras when they take you to the place of silence because you aren't thinking out the words; they are just coming from memory (like the Hail Mary for Catholics). One other thing: Grandpapa's greatest interest in philosophy is philosophy of religion, so ask him to help you understand concepts and writers like Tillich as you read.

About the squirrel image. Some people really get into their personality animal. The squirrel is happy, quick, industrious, busy, and always preparing for the next season, but she often forgets where she leaves her stored food. Does that sound like our Maggie? The important things the squirrel reminds us of are (1) plan for the future and be prepared for change (which you are doing); (2) slow down and focus to remember where you have stored your food for the "winter" (hmmmm . . . your prayer discussion); (3) try to have fun along the way and build trust where you did not have it before. The squirrel teaches us to gather our energies for the important tasks in life and to honor the future by preparing for change.

Sounds like you are "right on" with your choice of animal prototype! Keep it up, girl, and know we are praying for you each day.

Love You,
Nini

EHH, Monday, June 21, 2010

Dear Maggie,

Your latest journal entry shows great wisdom, not just intelligence. The truest prayer is indeed opening ourselves to God, consenting to God's presence, and consenting to be changed in the way God wants to change us—the God who is beyond all words.

Your story about the squirrels reminds me of a time when I was nine years old. I had gone with my mother and father (your great grandmother and great grandfather) to Birmingham for my mother to see a physician there. I was left in the car while they went in for the appointment. It was an old neighborhood, tree-covered and shady, and there were squirrels everywhere. I spent the whole time, maybe an hour and a half, just watching those squirrels. When my parents came back to the car, my father called the squirrels "gallanippers." That name has stuck with me for the past sixty-two years. There's no particular point to the story except that I like that name "gallanipper" and it was then that the breast cancer that killed my mother was discovered.

Back to Tolkien's *Lord of the Rings*, Nini and I were remembering that the book continues Gandalf's wisdom about deciding what to do with the time that's given us:

> He [Bilbo] used to say there was only one Road; that it was like a great river: its springs were at every doorstep, and every path was its tributary. "It's a dangerous business, Frodo, going out of your door," he used to say. "You step into the Road, and if you don't keep your feet, there is no knowing where you might be swept off to. Do you realize that this is the very path that goes through Mirkwood, and that if you let it, it might take you to the Lonely Mountain or even further and to worse places?" He used to say that on the path

outside the front door at Bag End, especially after he had been out for a long walk.[2]

It seems to me that we have no choice about stepping out of our front doors and into the Road. Life is treacherous. But it looks to me that you are keeping your feet awfully well!

As you probably know, Tolkien was a devout Roman Catholic. He said that he did not realize, when he was writing the first draft, that *The Lord of the Rings* was essentially an expression of Christian wisdom, but he saw it when he began to polish it for publication. At that point he became more deliberate in developing its theological themes.

Nini and I are coming to see you soon.

Love,

Grandpapa

---

2. Ibid., 72–73.

Why, God?

EHH

It was Fourth of July weekend when Nini and I made our first trip to visit Maggie and her mother Ellie at St. Jude. Her stepfather, Paul, and little sister, Flynn, were also there that weekend, and Maggie was doing well enough between treatments to enjoy going out to eat with us, showing us the ropes at St. Jude, and introducing us to some of the young patients and their families who were also living at Target House.

While there, Ellie told us about messages Maggie was receiving from people who wanted to encourage her, people who were truly concerned to help her. However, their messages assured her that there is a divine plan for everything that happens, even for all the pain and suffering in life. The implication of this way of thinking about God's way with the world is that God deliberately causes bad things in order to get good things and has, therefore, caused Maggie's cancer and the cancer of all the young patients she was meeting. In practical terms, this means that Maggie should rest in the assurance that God has given her Ewing's sarcoma for her own good. Here is God as the Grand Cosmic Designing Engineer who controls every detail of every life, meting out pain and pleasure, misery and happiness according to a mysterious and eternal blueprint. I myself may have thought so of God at one time, but I have been unable to think of God that way since my mother died of breast cancer when I was only thirteen. I now believe that this idea of God, stressing God's coercive power over God's love, is mistaken, and it is not the only way to understand God as creator and redeemer of the world.

Maggie was not having the Cosmic Engineer idea of God. Indeed, she later wrote that "there are few things I detest more than the saying that everything happens for a reason."

MCC, TUESDAY, JUNE 29, 2010

I have just completed three chemo treatments. I have twelve to go. If all goes as planned, I will be done with therapy around Christmas. My body has been responding really well to the chemo, so we will continue to do treatments every other week (most kids do it every three weeks). All in all, the reports have been good. And besides having to take twelve pills every morning, rinse with two mouthwashes, and drink Mirolax, my life is pretty good.

I met another patient yesterday. His name is Odie. He has liver cancer and lung cancer and his treatment plan is an experimental plan. Basically, he's one of those kids only a miracle can save. It hurts to see people like that. It hurts to see little innocent beautiful children suffering through chemotherapy. Because it's not their fault.

I think I have decided that everything does not happen for a reason. Everything cannot happen for a reason. Because there are hundreds of children in this building, and they don't get to experience childhood the way my sisters and I did. They walk up and down the halls, sometimes pushing their wheelchairs like walkers, sometimes leaning over crutches. They all have ports or lines so that people can take their blood from them every day and give them drugs that same way. It's not fair. It's not ok. It's not going to be ok. They lose their hair, and some of them hold onto every last strand, looking like rag dolls with a few strands of hair. They lose their appetites, and most days they vomit. They don't get to go to school or enjoy the summer or play sports or see their friends or have slumber parties. They can't go home, so this place becomes home. And I think that's kind of sad, that after a certain amount of time this lifestyle becomes normal and even nothing to be upset about. I hope that Odie gets better. I hope every kid I pass by gets better. But I know some of them won't. And I know that *that* doesn't happen for a reason.

I spend a lot of my time lying in bed and looking up at the ceiling. The ceiling is white and really offers no outlet for my creativity. But I look past it. I see a time and a place far away from here in which I, patient number 32455, am a real person again, a time when I can walk again, enjoy food again, sit in the heat, swim, and look at Facebook without getting jealous of every person who doesn't have to go through this. And when this time comes, which it will, I will be much, much more thankful for every little thing. And one day, I will be able to lie down on my bed at home and sleep peacefully, knowing that I am well.

Until then, I guess I get by by reminding myself of kids like Odie, kids that barely have a chance but have the ability to smile anyway. I am one of the lucky ones. I am going to be okay.

EHH

Not only could Maggie not believe in a God who singled her out for cancer in the Great Cosmic Blueprint, she could not believe it for the sake of Odie, whom only a miracle could save, or for the sake of the "hundreds of children in this building" suffering through chemotherapy, some of whom would die without ever experiencing a normal childhood.

While we were driving home to Baton Rouge, Nini and I discussed what we could do to help Maggie with her faith questions. We believed that she needed the support only God can give, but the idea of God being urged upon her by some was the idea of a god at best indifferent and at worst sadistic. Maggie could not accept it; neither could Nini and I. How could such a god be God?

Nini encouraged me to begin an email conversation with Maggie about faith matters. Here was one little thing I could do. It might also be helpful to Ellie, for she was in the middle of this struggle every bit as much as her daughter. My objective would be to respond to Maggie's questions and to remove obstacles to faith by telling a different story. For Christian faith offers a deep and rich understanding and way of life, one that enables us to enter into life with the God who has created all things and all worlds as an act of utterly generous love. It is the story of God saving and perfecting what God has created, even though the created order cannot but include random change, conflicts between creatures, misuses of freedom, terrible violence, and the suffering and death that follow.

For her part, Maggie was not going to let her search for God end with the unacceptable idea of the All-Knowing, All-Powerful Engineer-of-All. As she said, "Giving up on God without a thorough search was just as silly as believing in God without a thorough search." The search began in earnest at St. Jude. Part of the search would be intellectual, a search for a better way of thinking about God, a better idea of God. Toward this end and in addition to the faith conversation Maggie and I would have, there would be several other voices: her St. Jude chaplain Lisa Anderson, my son and Maggie's uncle, Carlisle Henderson, and Sam Martin, a family friend and Presbyterian minister.

MCC, JUNE, 2011

I could have given up on God and the idea of God, but I didn't. It wasn't fear that kept me from closing off my mind to the possibility of God; in my mind, giving up on God without a thorough search was just as silly as believing in God without a thorough search. One of the first places I began my search was at St. Jude. I had the option of speaking to a chaplain, and after a brief conversation with my psychologist, I was matched up with Lisa Anderson. The first time I met with Lisa, I came right out with my biggest concern. I asked her how she could possibly believe in a god when children and babies all around her were being diagnosed with cancer. I asked her how she could worship a god who did such things to people.

I don't remember the exact words Lisa used to answer my first questions, but I do remember her demeanor. To my surprise, she didn't look offended, disgusted, or angry. She smiled a little and looked at me, her eyes full of understanding. She said that after being around children with cancer and their families, after witnessing what they had to go through and watching them come out alive and happy and okay, she had to believe in God. Basically, she said that the strength and courage people showed was so amazing and so powerful that it had to have come from God, from out of this world. Children could get through cancer and chemo, and that was proof enough for her. I thought for a little while about what Lisa told me, and I thought I understood it, but I didn't. I couldn't. I hadn't experienced cancer yet. I hadn't seen others experience it. It was only later, after I had experienced cancer myself, that I could fully understand what Lisa meant.

My favorite thing about Lisa was that she was not judgmental. No matter what beliefs I proclaimed or toyed with, Lisa understood. She celebrated my curiosity instead of trying to contain it. She listened to my problems and let me cry about things to her in her office. She sometimes even rewarded me by telling me about some of her problems. She helped me to realize that a journey of faith is lifelong and continuous. All of my questions will never be answered, I realized, and Lisa helped me find a way to be okay with that.

Lisa also had stories to tell, true events that she'd witnessed as a chaplain. As she told me about the miracles she'd seen, I began to recognize miracles that occurred in my life on a day-to-day basis, even on the worst days. God, I realized, was more than I'd given God credit for. God didn't have to fit the molds of my childhood faith. God didn't have to be a man in the sky causing everything that happened in life. God could be found all around me. God was in the rain and the sun, the children laughing, and the love that shone all around me.

During my time at St. Jude, I also began to correspond with three men that I viewed as especially faithful and religious. The first of these was my Uncle Carlisle, my mother's brother, whom I'd always been close to. During my stay at St. Jude, Uncle Carlisle began writing me letters, and I responded with some of my questions about his religious beliefs and thoughts about my own. At the same time, I directed my questions to Grandpapa, my mother's father, who is a philosophy professor.

On many occasions, my grandfather, my uncle, and I shared an ongoing conversation addressing whether or not everything in life "happens for a reason." I found it extremely hard to believe that God would cause cancer just to teach people lessons. If God gave everyone cancer to teach them lessons or fulfill purposes, then why did people die from it? Why couldn't they learn lessons and then live?

Another thing we discussed was whether or not cancer was a punishment. Had I done something to deserve it? As ignorant as this question may sound, I actually struggled with it. There were times when I felt guilty because I'd gotten cancer. I felt like something must have separated me from the people who don't get cancer. If sin caused cancer, though, then what about the children who had cancer? What about the babies who were born with cancer?

In the end, though, Grandpapa and Uncle Carlisle helped me to rule out the possibility that God has a "reason" for my cancer. God didn't *give* me cancer. It just happened. What mattered, was how I dealt with my cancer.

The third person I corresponded with about religion (and many other things, for that matter) was Sam Martin, a good friend of my family's, who

I like to refer to as my "adopted grandfather." A Presbyterian minister, Sam suggested that God is to be found most clearly in the relationships of people with each other. "Holy things don't drop down on heavenly parachutes," Sam said. "They come to life in human interaction. God lives in the space between people who care for each other." This idea resonated in me, reminding me of what Lisa had said: God is most evident in people, in the way they connect, in the way they love, and in the way they cope. By that definition, my experiences with cancer were full of God.

I am still in ongoing discussions about faith and religion with my uncle and grandfather. Perhaps the most valuable thing they have taught me is that there are many beliefs and belief systems within Christianity. There are many answers to my questions. Sometimes, it is not the answers that matter; it is the searching for them.

EHH

Thankfully, then, Maggie was hearing wise voices, not voices telling her to trust in a god who had decided to give her cancer. Nevertheless, she remained unsure about what to think about God and did not think of herself as a person of faith, even though her early journal entries speak of having faith and reveal an understanding and practice of prayer more profound than most attain until they have lived many more than her nineteen years. The journal entries also reveal an attitude of trust and compassion. At the very least, Maggie was open to the possibility of an actively present and loving God.

On our return from Memphis, I initiated our faith conversation.

EHH, Tuesday, July 7, 2010.

I want to begin a conversation with you about your experience and the confusion you feel about what to believe. I just read a message to you on Facebook from an adult friend. It said that her seven-year-old little sister was hit and killed by a car because God wanted her in heaven with Him! Yikes! I think that theology, that way of understanding bad things that happen, is awful. If I thought God went around deciding to give people cancer or causing them to be killed in accidents or causing tsunamis to strike and kill thousands of people, and so on and on, then I would not have faith in that god. Even if I believed such a god exists, I wouldn't feel I had any reason to love and trust that god.

Of course, someone who has had cancer or lost a little sister may find that way of thinking about it somehow comforting. Nevertheless, I think they're working with some bad theology. Their bad theology doesn't nullify their faith because, as St. Augustine recognized centuries ago, having faith does not mean that one knows the truth about God. Faith is an attitude of trusting and depending on God and of *seeking* understanding. But I don't think they've found a very good way of understanding God.

Here's what I believe. God did not single you out and give you cancer as part of a plan for you and in order to test you or teach you something and certainly not to punish you. God does, on the other hand, create the kind of world in which cancer and all kinds of other destructive things happen. I think that's because the world would not really be a real world if it did not have room for those terrible things. While the way faithful people understand God is important, their faithful living relationship with God is far more important. But God does want us to trust that no matter what happens, God cares about us and will redeem all that has happened. I believe that one of the lessons of the crucifixion and resurrection of Christ is that God suffers with us and will ultimately redeem our suffering. So Frederick Buechner suggests that God says "Here is the world. Beautiful and terrible things will happen. Don't be afraid. I am with you. Nothing can ever separate us."[1]

On the other hand, when bad things happen, there is always a faithful response to be made, and it is in the faithful responses that we can see God acting. That doesn't mean God is not acting in other ways, but it is in faithful and obedient dependence on God and in loving actions on behalf of others that we can most clearly experience God acting. Where your cancer is concerned, I see God acting in your own tenacity, courage, and determination, in your mother's heroic and courageous love and caretaking, in the dedicated work of nurses and doctors, in those who give money to St Jude and those who give their time to come teach the classes in Japanese, guitar, and knitting which you and Flynn are enjoying. I see God acting in the many messages and visits you receive from friends who know you and even from those who don't, as they encourage you and try their best to say or do something that will help you.

1. Buechner, *Listening to Your Life*, 289.

I visit the Louisiana State Penitentiary at Angola. Some of the men there have done awful, awful things: rape and murder, for instance. But I don't for one second think God planned for them to become criminals, all for some purpose God had for them. Some of the men at Angola who have become Christians might think that their murdering someone was itself part of a plan by God to get them to Angola where they could be converted. But, of course, I don't think that idea is true. More important than the way they think about it is that they have become persons of faith. Being persons of faith means they have the confidence that in spite of what they've done and in spite of anything bad that happens to them, God loves them and is making them the persons God created them to be. And it means that they can trust in and depend on God. They have become very different people. That's amazing. And that's something I wholeheartedly believe really is the kind of thing God can do in persons. God's hands are always, always on us, trying in whatever circumstances there are to make us into people who love God with all our being and our neighbors as ourselves. The more we choose to cooperate and try, the more God can do. And that, I believe, is what faith is about.

God does not cause bad things to happen to us in order to teach us something; yet no matter what happens, it is always possible to learn from and respond faithfully to bad things. I think that's what St. Paul meant when he said that "in all things God works for the good of those who love him . . ." (Romans 8:28) That doesn't mean the bad stuff never happened or that it happened in order for God to do something good with it. It means that there is always a faithful response that gets good out of the bad. The faithful response lets God pick up the broken pieces and mend them, pick up broken people and make them whole.

The crucifixion and resurrection are the primary Christian examples of this. Some Christians think that God planned for Jesus to be crucified so that he could be the "payment" for our sins. The "payment" idea is a particular image for understanding how Christ puts persons at one with God. For many years I thought that was literally the one belief that makes one a Christian. While I still believe that it is through his crucifixion and resurrection that Christ puts us at one with God, I no longer think "payment" is the best image for thinking about it or understanding it. On the other hand, others, myself among them, believe that God's desire was that we would recognize Jesus's life as the living and active presence of God, the very reign or kingdom of God set among us, and that we would join in and participate in his incarnation of divine life. Instead, we humans, even we religiously devout humans, rejected Jesus's faithful and obedient life and executed him. So Christ was crucified, and God raised him to divine life, turning our failure into God's salvation by making his obedient faithfulness accessible to us. In this way, then, the crucifixion and resurrection, which are the heart of Christianity, are the supreme instance of God's turning bad things to good ends.

I could go on, but this is more than enough for now. I'm sending you a little book called *Quarks, Chaos and Christianity*, by John Polkinghorne. He was a particle physicist at Cambridge, involved in the discovery of quarks and gluons. Later in his life he became an Anglican priest and theologian. He writes very clearly and, because of his background in science, with a lot of authority. If you want to think about why the world is the kind of world in which bad stuff happens and why God doesn't just wipe all the bad stuff out, this book is a good place to start.

MCC, MONDAY, JULY 19, 2010.

I am very excited to be starting this conversation with you. I hope that I can find something that you have so much of: faith. Grandpapa, I don't have faith. I don't think I've ever had faith. I know that I have wonder, though. I wonder a lot, far too much actually. I wonder about blood types and tree types and cancer types and types of religions. I wonder about gods and the invisible and the visible and if what I am seeing is real. I wonder about life. I wonder about death. I also feel a lot. I feel for people and animals and even plants. Perhaps the only thing that keeps me hoping for God is my ability to feel. Sometimes I even feel too much.

You wrote about how I was thinking of God as giving me cancer and how you don't believe in that type of God. I don't, either. The God of the Hebrew Bible, Yahweh, seems like a mean, angry god. I refuse to worship anything that mean. I don't even believe in hell, in any sense of the word. I don't love that god.

I like the way you talk about God as comfort in times of hardship, as tenacity and courage during my cancer. I think I see that sometimes, like when I get to make a little kid with liver cancer smile for half a second, or when I'm in a room full of people who love me and I can't stop bursting with love. But how do I know that those aren't just good human feelings produced by chemical reactions in the brain? I know that you can't give me proof. No one can give me proof.

I didn't know that you believed what you do about Jesus. I assumed that all "Christians" believed Jesus was supposed to die for us; that that was what God planned for him from the beginning. I am relieved to know that I don't have to believe that. I learned a lot at school last year about the construction of the Bible. The Gospels were written forty years after the death of Jesus. Paul's letters were about twenty years after Jesus's death. Instead of making me more cynical, I found it sort of amazing that a group of people could carry a tradition so far past the death of one man. And I think that the historical Jesus was who we should aim to be. So maybe I am already thinking like a Christian, just not like the ones around here. But here is where things get hardest for me.

If God is as loving and wonderful as Jesus (which he or she must be in order for me to like him or her), how can God punish anyone for seeking a life of faith? Aren't Islam and Hinduism and Buddhism and Judaism and Christianity all the same thing? Aren't we all just people trying our best to reach out and touch something a little bit bigger than we are? If God condemns people for believing in a different way than I believe, I can't believe in God.

Is God perfect or not? Is God all powerful or not? Clearly, if I have cancer, God makes mistakes. Or are you a deist? That is, do you believe God made the world and now nature plays out and God does not interfere?

I know I have a lot of questions, and they probably don't all have answers, but thank you so much for trying to answer them. Thank you for wanting to have this discussion with me. This is the best gift you could ever give me.

EHH

Because Maggie said she did not have faith, I thought comments about the nature of faith were in order. I wrote as follows.

EHH, Wednesday, July 21, 2010

Dear Maggie,

The common idea about faith is that "faith" means believing something is true, even though there are no reasons to believe it and even though there are reasons to the contrary: "believing six impossible things before breakfast," in Lewis Carroll's memorable phrase. This way of understanding treats faith as a special kind of knowledge. Faith does have a knowledge dimension, but knowledge is not its essence. Think about faith in a person. When we have faith in a person, it is based on knowing the person and what the person is like, so it has a knowledge component. But the kind of knowing involved is not the kind of knowing you might get from putting the person through a battery of medical or psychological tests.

Apply that to religious faith. You mentioned in your journal that your grandmother Anne had given you a book by Paul Tillich to help you with your questions about faith. Tillich is an excellent place to begin. He describes faith as the attitude of being ultimately concerned about something—or you could say "ultimately devoted" to something. That means that devotion to that something comes before everything else, that everything else takes a back seat to it, that the devotion defines the way one's life goes. In that very broad sense of faith, one can have faith in, say, the United States of America or in a political party or in a particular church organization. To give such objects one's ultimate devotion is to make them one's god and to worship them. But they are not truly God. Only God, who is beyond all understanding, is truly ultimate and worthy of faith or ultimate devotion.

Unfortunately, religious people are prone to idolatry in the sense that we tend to form our own understandings of the ultimate reality, which we call God, and then to forget that our understanding is something imperfect and always in need of correction and improvement. So we worship our own idea of God as though the idea itself were God when it's actually something partly made up by us. To avoid this we have to remind ourselves that we are finite, confess that we don't perfectly know the truth, and do our best to keep the ultimacy of God in our minds and our minds open to corrected and improved understanding.

I think it's possible not to be aware of what one is ultimately devoted to and, therefore, not to know what one actually worships. I also think it's possible to be in a state of searching for what to regard as ultimately real and ultimately most important. And that's where I think you are now. You haven't decided. That's wonderful. You are a seeker! Those who seek will find. Indeed, perhaps in seeking you have already found, even if you don't realize it yet.

That's enough for now. Although I'm not going to try to impose my beliefs on you, I will try to tell you what I think and why, and I will try to do it as clearly as I can. It will involve explaining that faith in the more particular sense of Christian faith is properly not as much a set of beliefs as it is a way of life. Beliefs are important to it. The way of life called 'faith' needs to keep improving its understanding so that it can be lived well. This is true for all religions; they are all ways of life that make use of particular ways of understanding. Now, if God is the ultimate reality and is best understood as personal (or as *at least* personal, *not less than* personal), then the way of life that is the life of faith is going to be more like interpersonal life than it is like knowing calculus, chemistry, or history. That is, Christian faith will be more on the order of personal friendship, loyalty and devotion. The ultimate reality God will be understood as a reality to which ultimate devotion and loyalty are owed.

EHH

By this time the brutality of the treatments was beginning to take a toll. Maggie was still writing in her journal, but discomfort, pain, uncertainty, and the other feelings that pressed upon her made it hard for her to think about the conceptual matters of our faith conversation. I wrote again, responding to her journal rather than to a new letter from her.

EHH, Sunday, August 8, 2010.

Dear Maggie,

A lot has happened since our last exchange, and I have a feeling that some of the questions that were on your mind before may no longer be pressing. What I read in your journal tells me that you are very much on the road of faith. Your experience has, so to speak, thrown you like Frodo out your front door step and onto a road rife with challenges. You have embraced the journey and are well along the way. What makes it confusing is that it may not be what most people think of when they speak of faith. It's just so common to think that faith is a matter of believing ideas, of thinking that certain ideas are true. But that doesn't seem to be what Jesus meant by 'faith' when he said 'Your faith has made you whole.' But you are walking now through the uncertainties and accidents of your life in an attitude of expectation, confidence, acceptance, trust, and joy in the midst of and in spite of the pain, suffering, and fear you are bound to be feeling.

You are on the journey of faith. When in your journal you mention that you feel confident, proud of yourself in an "I'm fighting cancer to win and I love myself for the first time in my life," when you say you wish you could take Odie's tumors away, when you see God in nine people sitting around you, and when you think prayer is not having perfect words but being open and willing to think and feel as deeply as you can: these things and more make it plain to me that you are walking this road of life deliberately and passionately and with a determination most of us can barely begin to understand.

Thinking about faith some more, I'm reminded of what my friend Diogenes Allen said about it. He said that faith is being willing to receive the good God intends for us and that the good God intends is that we be transformed into persons who love God with all our being and our neighbors as ourselves.[2] Faith in this sense also means being willing to suffer whatever may come when we consent to being changed. Add to that the effort to cooperate with God's desire to accomplish those changes in us and we've got a pretty complete statement of what faith is. Better than that, your life right now demonstrates what it is.

You asked how anyone can be punished for seeking God in a different religion or for believing in a non-Christian way? I assume you ask that question because you know Christians who think that faith involves believing that God punishes people who don't believe as Christians do. Well, I think you are right not to believe that. I don't either, although I believed it in an earlier time of my life. My faith's way of understanding tells me that being a lover and follower of Jesus does not require me to believe that. I think that those Christians or Muslims (or whatever group you want to name) who really believe that only those who understand God in their particular way can be "saved" are flat-out wrong; they are treating their *beliefs* as their God. They are treating their beliefs as though they were the most important reality there is, as though their beliefs are the reality to which they owe their ultimate devotion. That's dangerously close to idolatry. Such idolatry is, of course, a universal human tendency. We all want to think we've got the final and most important truth. You and I are going to do our best not to fall into that trap.

As we've said before, faith seeks understanding, and it has unfortunately become a common way of understanding faith to think of God as a punisher of souls for thinking and doing the "wrong" things or belonging

2. Allen, *Christian Belief*, chapter 6.

to the "wrong" religion. But even Dante, who wrote about hell, did not think that God puts people in hell. He thought of hell as a condition people prefer to be in and choose, as a state that one's way of life puts one in. God is always at work in persons trying to move them onto the path of love—and, I believe, that effort doesn't end when someone dies. God will still have his "making hands" on us.[3] So we might as well give ourselves into God's hands and cooperate with God's gracious action. In Christian terms that's what believing in Christ is; it's believing that the God who lovingly endures the suffering thrown up by the world and who gives himself over into our hands is always there at work trying to get us into his life of eternal and unconditional love. Well, whether you have thought about it that way or not, that's the life of faith, the journey you're on. It's not about fear and punishment; it's about confidence and joy and being part of the life of God.

You also asked whether I think God is perfect? All-powerful? If all-powerful, then isn't cancer a mistake? Although not all Christians think about these things in the same way (and that should be a comforting thought), I will tell you what I think.

Yes, I believe God is perfect. I think St. Anselm came as close as possible to saying in abstract philosophical terms what God is. He said that whatever else may be true about God, God is the being "than which no greater (or better or more perfect) can be conceived" or that God is "the absolutely perfect being."[4]

Now, we human beings tend to assume that we know what 'perfect' means, but we can be quite wrong about that. We naturally think about perfection in terms of what we might wish for ourselves, and that's likely to be the power to do whatever we want and the power to prevent any evil from occurring and to correct any evil that exists. But the Christian religion suggests something different. Christians take Jesus as the revelation of God. If we want to know what God is like, we must look to Jesus. So if that is true, what does it tell us? Well, it doesn't tell us that God goes around overpowering everything to always make things go the way God wants or the way we want. On the contrary, God in Jesus makes God's own Self subject to the world. God, then, suffers at the hands of the world and from its accidents and unpredictabilities and catastrophes—and especially at our hateful hands.

3. Farrer, *Austin Farrer*, 208.
4. Anselm, *Basic Writings*, 7.

Christianity tells us that God's perfection consists primarily in God's love. God is perfect self-giving love, always perfectly given, perfectly received, perfectly returned, and perfectly shared—all within the very life God enjoys, even apart from God's engagement with us. Why should we think that? I think it's because the life of perfect love is the best life we can imagine. And if God is the most perfect life, then the best way we can imagine God is as one who always enacts and experiences the perfection of love within God's own life and as one who desires that all created things freely share in that life of perfect-love-in-action.

What God's perfect loving of creation cannot allow is that creation be overridden and forced to follow an idea or plan in God's mind. If that were the way God acted in the world, the world would not be real in itself; it would be a figment of divine imagination, God's intentional dream or God's self-produced DVD, as it were. So, I think that in creating the world, in choosing to have a world instead of just being all that there is, God has to limit God's coercive power. God has to let the world be itself, but as Farrer, Polkinghorne, and others argue, God patiently works from the bottom up and through the process of evolution to get a world that includes creatures who are able to be free and who can recognize the presence of divine action in the reality of love. For such a real world, the kind of world we find ourselves living in, God must wait for us to recognize and to respond to God's love. God must wait for us to throw in with the divine love, to cooperate with it, and to consent to being transformed by it into persons who love God with all our hearts, with all our souls, with all our minds, and with all our strength—and our neighbors as ourselves. That's what I see in Christ, the active presence of that eternal love made clear and present, so that I can "latch onto it"—latch onto him—and be made part of it, part of him, part of the joyful life of God and so live in the kingdom of heaven.

I am sure that people recognize and respond to that love not only in Christian terms but also in the terms and practices of other religions, but I describe the way Christians think and understand. It's the way I have learned and the way that lets me receive the most help from others, since there are lots of others around me who are also traveling the road in the light of the stories of Jesus and with the help of Jesus.

Finally, am I a deist? No! I believe that God has always been and will always be active in the world God has created. You have noticed the ways in which God is most clearly active now by noticing God acting in the love your friends and family express, in the staff at St. Jude, and in your patient-friends like Odie. I see God acting in you, in your mother and all your family, in your friends, and in the nurses and doctors, etc. No, God is very much active in the world.

I'm glad you all went to St. Mary's, met Andy Andrews, and had a good experience. And, by the way, the tears you shed? I think they are a sign of God's presence. Nini and I are coming back around the end of this month, a few days before you'll be having the surgery. We hope you'll be feeling like it and that we can all go to St. Mary's together—after eating dinner on Saturday with all of you.

Nini and I love you, Maggie, and I'm glad we're getting to know each other this way. I know what you mean in saying that you're no hero, that you're not brave. Nevertheless, you are an inspiration to us and we see your heroism and bravery whether you feel it or not.

EHH

Maggie's life at St. Jude was about to enter its fourth month, and things were going well. Her hopes were high that tests would show her ready for the surgery that would remove the cancer from her leg and let her begin life again, let her complete the remaining chemo treatments that would finish off the cancer for good, and let her learn to walk with an internal titanium prosthesis. But life was not easy. Maggie was being stretched to the limit. From our faith perspective, she was on a cross, and it was not fun.

MCC, SATURDAY, AUGUST 21, 2010.

I just finished my sixth chemo treatment, and I recently got back a lot of good reports from my scans. I should be excited. I should be looking for the light at the end of the tunnel and making way too many plans for when I'm healthy again. But I'm having trouble with that right now. This last chemo was bad, really bad. It was the most torturous thing I have ever been through. I feel tired, sick, and run down. I feel like my body has been attached to four separate eighteen-wheelers and dragged across the ground. It hurts to eat. It hurts to turn over in bed, and it hurts more than anything to think about my next chemo treatment. I should be excited: my surgery is right around the corner (September 2), I'm halfway done with therapy, and all my friends are moving back to school at Rhodes. But I'm terrified. I'm so terrified and vulnerable and hurt. I've found out the hard way that chemotherapy has a cumulative effect, so I don't expect my physical pains to get any better. But I have to find strength in something, in someone, in some piece of myself. I have to find a way not to give up.

If you haven't heard the good news, here it is. My first MRI since diagnosis came back and showed one centimeter off the tumor both ways. My PET scan, which picks up glucose levels in the body and basically shows where the live cancer is in the whole body, just barely picked up a little on one side of my leg. My heart is still healthy. My kidneys are in good condition. I should be thrilled. I should be rejoicing. And I was for a few days until I became a victim of chemotherapy once again.

So here's what I'm going to do now. I'm going to write down all the things that make me who I am, all the things that are Maggie, all the things that inspire me to be better and stronger. Memories. People. Words. Poems. I'm hoping that this will allow me to find myself in the places where Maggie is hard to find—in the chemo, in the nausea, and in the lack of energy, in the hospital beds, over the trash-cans puking, missing school—because I'm not ready to give up. No matter how hard it is, I am going to beat this disease.

MCC, SUNDAY, SEPTEMBER 5, 2010

I am glad to hear you are not a deist. And I really liked your response to my question about God's power and limitations. "All-powerful" seems to me to be a very tricky and philosophical phrase. I guess it all depends on how we define "all-powerful" or "perfect." And it seems to me that maybe really being a Christian (not in the way most people today who claim to be Christian are) is not about judging other religions or condemning people to hell or gaining a way to heaven. Maybe really being a Christian is defining "perfection" and "all-powerful" as what Christ was.

I have to wonder, though, whether Abraham represents the same thing for Jews and Muhammad for Muslims. From what I have studied about these religions, it seems like the Christians worshipped Christ as a part of God, and the other faith communities only regarded their leaders as prophets. Why do you think Christ was different? Do you think Muhammad was sent to the Islamic peoples in the same way Jesus was sent to the Israelites? Do you think God—whatever God is—sent Muhammad? Is it possible that Hinduism and Buddhism are also ways of reaching the same thing: God, spirituality. How can any type of spirituality be rejected? And am I a Christian if I believe that all religions are good? I know you have sort of answered some of these questions. "Faith seeks understanding." I think I am very good at understanding different religions and beliefs, but I wonder sometimes if I am too understanding. Perhaps it is because our society is often not understanding. I just can't see how human attempts to be spiritual can be wrong.

When I saw you last, I think I told you a little about that way I've been meditating. I think I have been able to connect with God. I told my chaplain that I didn't like praying with words because I felt like words close God in and make God something like the way mainstream Christians present God (when I say 'mainstream Christians,' I mean the ones that are judging, condemning, closed-minded, etc.). But it's really hard to think without the use of language. In a sense, we are our language. Meditation, though, allows me to connect with God without using language. Sometimes I choose one word, like 'peace' or 'platelets' and think about it over and over again. Sometimes I just imagine being healthy again. Sometimes I imagine Odie being healthy or Flynn being really happy. Sometimes I just feel whatever it is I'm feeling—like anger or sadness or relief or fear. Sometimes I imagine my cancer shrinking. And sometimes in the midst of these meditations, I feel calm. I feel relief. I feel comfort. I feel hope. I feel happiness. I feel at peace. And I think that this is God.

What bothers me most right now is that most 'Christians' would read this email and consider it heretical. Most 'Christians' don't seem to be understanding or Christ-like. How did this happen? I know that I shouldn't be concerned with what other people think about my faith, but faith is something that should be shared, right?

I am so excited that we are getting closer, and I want you to know how much I love you.

EHH

Not knowing when the surgery was at last to be done, I wrote my next contribution on September 6, which turned out to be surgery day, though I did not know that at the time.

EHH, Monday, September 6, 2010.

First, here are my short answers to the concerns you expressed in your last addition to the conversation.

1. No, I do not think that other forms of spirituality, either in different branches of Christianity or in different religions, are necessarily wrong. But see 2 below.

2. And, yes, it is true that many who consider themselves Christians are judgmental, condemning, and closed-minded. Some of those are not malicious or vicious about it; they have just been educated into an unhelpful way of understanding faith and may in life be quite generous; others may be mean-spirited about it. The same is true about adherents of other religions, because all people tend to take their most precious beliefs and use them to assure themselves that they have the truth and thereby to set themselves above others who do not, they think, have the truth. But that's a misuse of religion, not a proper use of it.

3. Do Christians believe that Christ is "part of God"? Not exactly "part" of God." But most do think about Jesus differently from the way Jews think about Abraham or Moses and Muslims about Mohammed. What Christians believe is that Christ is the eternal Son of God who in Jesus of Nazareth lived the perfect love of God for the World but lived it within the limits and circumstances of human life. It's impossible to explain this doctrine of incarnation in a completely satisfying way, but the best way, I think, is to take it in terms of its practical or "live-able" meaning. In practical terms, to say that Christ is both God and man, both divine and human, means that in Jesus the Christ we see who the mysterious God is. Do you want to know what God is like and how God acts? Then look at Jesus of Nazareth.

4. Believing that other forms of spirituality are good does not make you a heretic.

5. The kinds of meditation you describe are real modes of prayer, genuine ways of relating to God.

Your latest response (September 5) tells me that the heart of your worries about Christian faith have much to do with the attitude of exclusivity and condemnation that many Christians do express. "Mainstream Christians," you say, are those who are "judging, condemning, and closed-minded." You cannot see how any human attempts to be spiritual can be wrong, and what bothers you most is that most Christians would read your last email and consider it "heretical." Also related to the attitude of exclusivity that bothers you about Christians is their idea that Christ is special, not just a prophet but "a part of God," and that non-Christian forms of spirituality must, therefore, be wrong. Barbara Brown Taylor's *An Altar in the World*, which Nini and I sent you, will give you a different perspective. Not all Christians would agree that other forms of belief and spirituality are wrong. And I hope that that is not truly the "mainstream of Christianity."

What is it about the understanding of some Christians that makes Christianity seem judgmental, condemning, and closed-minded? I suspect it is the following:

1. The evangelistic emphasis: You must "believe in Jesus Christ as your personal Lord and Savior," or you will go to hell; therefore (this mind-set goes), since other religions do not involve believing in Jesus Christ, their adherents must be condemned to hell.

2. The insistence by some churches that in order to attain salvation you must believe as they do and accept the church's complete authority (in other words, those who don't will go to hell).

3. Along with these authoritative claims is the frequent mention of John 14:6. "I am the way and the truth and the life; no one comes to the Father except by me."

Let's divide and conquer.

First, take the "going to hell" part. Again, the popular understanding of this does not match well with the best of what theologians have said over the centuries, though there certainly have been a lot of examples of priests and preachers who have pressed the usual condemning way of understanding. In the popular mind, "going to hell" means getting sent to hell by God as the eternal pay-back for not believing in God in the right way, for not thinking a certain way or for not thinking that certain ideas are true, and for un-repented wrongful behavior. Church people have certainly been willing to use such a way of thinking to try to "*scare* the hell out of people"—and to control them and get them to support the institution, etc. Humans are humans, and they (we) do want to control other people. They (we) may even do it thinking sincerely that they are helping them. While the greatest Christian thinking about hell is in the writing of Dante and Milton, one Roman Catholic and the other Protestant, C. S. Lewis is closer to us in time and language and distills much classical wisdom in his way of imagining heaven and hell. One of the places where he does this is in his novel *The Great Divorce*.

Lewis represents hell imaginatively as a place where every inhabitant is doing what she wants and getting what she wants and yet is never happy with it. You might say that being unhappy is what makes them happy. Buses leave regularly for heaven. Most of the occupants of hell get into fights with each other and won't even get on the bus. And, again, most who do get on the bus and who arrive at the outer reaches of heaven, won't stay very long but get back on the bus in order to go back to the life, the "hell" they're comfortable with. They won't stay because they are not willing to receive the kind of happiness and life of love and service that they find when they get there. They prefer their old attitudes and the lives that go with them.

Heaven and hell, then, are not external conditions imposed on us by God. Rather, they are the internal being or the self-being we most fundamentally desire and choose for ourselves. So Dante, in fact, gives a picture of Satan not as the master of hell but as a pitiable spirit who is so completely malformed that he is isolated from all others and so frozen in ice that he cannot even weep. Heaven, on the other hand, he sees as a condition in which one has become someone who loves God and neighbor and, therefore, experiences continual joy in seeing others fulfilled and happy.

In addition to heaven and hell, Dante also writes about purgatory, and I think his picture of it is actually a wonderfully imaginative representation of what the life of faith is like in this world. Persons in Dante's imagined purgatory suffer, as we do. But they are "happy in the fire." They are happy because they accept that God intends their good, and they are willing to receive it instead of insisting on some other good of their own choosing. Remember Diogenes Allen's idea? Real faith requires consenting to or being willing to receive the good that God intends instead of insisting on the good we imagine for ourselves. In the life of faith, therefore, persons cooperate with God's grace (and 'grace' is another word for God's active presence), as well as they can understand it, by cooperating with God's loving action of trying to make them into lovers of God and neighbor. Dante represents the souls in purgatory (which I take to be persons who are now living the life of faith) as persons who help each other and have times of rest and joy along the way. They sing; they pray; they encourage each other and take pleasure in being together. They also get to rest, unlike Dante's souls in hell. In fact, their most dangerous tendency is to dilly dally along the way rather than to rush eagerly to cooperate with the grace that is trying to give them their real good.

And what is the good God intends? As we've said before, it is to be a person who in her own unique and distinctive way loves God with all her being and her neighbors as herself. The hope of heaven is the hope of being brought to such perfection.

I hope that these thoughts, these ways of understanding, will help in getting past the idea that Christianity is essentially a matter of believing that people who don't believe the Christian doctrines will be punished by God's sending them to hell in a great payback. Many Christians do charge that God will punish people in hell if they do not believe the Christian doctrines. Maybe most of us are judgmental and condemning at times. We ought not to be. Jesus himself told us not to judge. But persons of all religions manage somehow to take their very best wisdom and use it in a self-serving way, use it to set themselves self-righteously apart from others. It's the human-all-too-human trick of assuring ourselves that we're okay by cutting other people down. And it's the great danger in all religion: the use of religious beliefs and principles for the wrong purposes.

Does hell exist as an eternal condition of chosen misery? I don't think anyone knows. Perhaps God succeeds ultimately in getting everyone to become who God created them to be. But if there are those who resolutely and absolutely refuse to receive the good God intends for them, then I think God will relieve them of suffering by granting them oblivion, the complete cessation of existence and relief from misery.

Where does this leave us with the widely held interpretation that to be "saved" we must believe in or "accept Jesus Christ as personal Lord and Savior"? I hope what I've already said prepares us to understand those words better than I think many of the people who speak them actually do. I have not always thought of accepting Christ as I do now, and I do not claim to have nailed down the complete and final truth. However, it is the way my faith has found to understand at this late stage of my life. But, again, a living relationship with Christ is more important than the way we think about him, although how we think is important to the relationship. We hope for ways of thinking that help us in the relationship rather than getting in its way.

So what I now believe it means to accept and follow Christ as my Lord and Savior is not that I will be rewarded with heaven and saved from misery just by holding the right beliefs as true. "Believing" in the sense of "believing in Christ" is far more than thinking that the statement "Jesus is Lord and Savior" is a true statement—as though it were like thinking that $5 + 7 = 12$ is true. Believing in Christ as the way, truth, and life by whom one comes to the Father is more like believing in your mother as a person you can count on always to be there with you through your fight with this dreadful cancer. You know her; she has always been there fighting for you; and she will be there fighting for you no matter what she has to endure. You trust her; you look to her for comfort; and you are grateful to her. What would you do without her? That's the way truly believing in Christ is.

It should now make sense to say that salvation is an internal transformation of oneself that expresses itself in one's actual life with people in God's world. It means loving all persons; that is, it means really desiring the good God desires and wills for us all, being joyful when we see persons receiving it and being sad for them when we see them rejecting it for some false good.

And, again, what is the good God desires and wills for each person? It is that each one should become a person who loves God with their whole being and their neighbors as themselves—and does so as the particular and unique person she is. To be such a person is to be part of the very life of God, part of what God, because God is God, is always doing. Such incorporation into God's life is salvation. It is the beginning of heaven in the here and now. No matter what happens, one can rejoice in receiving that good.

Now, I do believe that the Gospel according to John has it right. Christ is the way, the truth, and the life because he is the one who lives the divine way in the very circumstances, conditions, and limits of human life, which we all must face. That is, he really does love God with all his being and his neighbors (including his enemies) as himself. He lives the desire for us to receive the good God intends for us. He lives the desire for us to be perfected as the unique persons God has made us to be. He shows us in his life what the good God intends for us is, and he shows us what receiving it requires of us. He is the instance of actually lived faith *par excellence*. Because he lives the perfect relationship of persons to God, Christians say that "Here is a divine man, a real man who is also the very love of God among us." He is the perfect love of God unfolded before us. What he does is what God does; the life that he lives is the life that God lives in the real conditions of the world. Living that life gets him crucified, and the crucifixion is done because the most "religious" people of his time are judgmental, condemning, and closed-minded. They (and it is what all of us religious people are in danger of doing) use their religion for the wrong purposes. But God raises him to new life. Thus, living the life of faith is not a way of making life easy and getting what we want short term; it is loving God and neighbors no matter what the short term consequences may be and trusting that God will make it good.

Authentically or truly believing in Christ is seeing in him who God is. It is loving God as the one who goes to death because of loving us and doing everything to help us to receive the good God desires for us. It is seeing God's eternal love being acted out in the realities of life and latching on to it. It is joining oneself to that active love of God as best one can in the assurance that, though we have not yet become persons who love God with all our being and our neighbors as ourselves, we are already connected in Christ to the eternal and perfect love that God is. Any kind of spirituality, any kind of belief that assists people in knowing and desiring that transformation and committing to it will be, I believe, "coming to the Father by Christ," and it will be good.

I believe that in Christ we have a wonderful advantage. In him we see the eternal love of God being lived before us and can not only understand the idea that God loves us unconditionally and adopt the principle of love as a principle to try to live by, but we can join ourselves to it, reach out and grab hold and receive God's help in receiving the good God desires for us.

I've written an awful lot of words, but doing so has given me the chance to find out what I think at this point of my life. Do remember that this is only "faith seeking understanding." Far more important is the willingness to be transformed into a lover of God and neighbor. I am painfully aware that my efforts to live this understanding are woefully deficient.

EHH

By the end of this long letter it seemed clear enough that Maggie was living well with her doubts. She was open, seeking, praying, sensing the presence of God, and being nurtured in a matrix which she came to know more and more as sacramental, as mediating to her the kingdom of heaven. She more and more recognized God's presence: hidden in the relationships with persons who loved her, hidden, yes, but actual and becoming more and more visible to her through eyes of faith.

Maggie and her family had endured the initial treatments. Now they waited for the surgery—waited with great hope but also with much apprehension.

6

Sacramental Experiences

EHH

In the months leading up to the surgery and while we were having our faith conversation by email, two experiences played especially important roles in Maggie's movement into a more intentional and focused life of faith. The first came with a visit to St. Mary's Episcopal Cathedral in Memphis, and it led to an ongoing counseling relationship with the cathedral dean, the Rev. Andy Andrews. The second began when she met another cancer patient at St. Jude, twelve-year-old Odie Harris from Bossier City, Louisiana.

These experiences were sacramental in the full sense of the word. They were ordinary events and actions involving ordinary flesh and blood persons, and they were at the same time actions of God mediating God's presence to Maggie. Now, if we humans were able to pay sufficient attention, we would be able to see the sacramental character of the whole of creation, for it is God's action in the created order that underlies its existence, makes it what it is, and sustains it in being. But, limited and insensitive as we humans are, we too often need special events to overtake us as having special importance because of the ways they connect with our deep cares and concerns. Then we can know them as special events and see God at work in them. So it was with Maggie's visit to St. Mary's on an ordinary Sunday morning in July, 2010, and with her waiting-room meeting with Odie.

There is irony in Maggie's first visit to St. Mary's, for a good part of her difficulty with Christian faith had to do with negative experiences and perceptions of churches and the people who frequent them. While I tried to say in our faith conversation that the closed-minded condemning attitude Maggie worried about is not properly part of being a faithful Christian, it was her actual experience of St. Mary's rather than any words or theological arguments that enabled her to receive grace through the church.

Nini and I had attended St. Mary's on our first trip to visit Maggie. We were excited to see Andy Andrews listed outside the cathedral as dean. We had known him as a curate in our home parish of St. James in Baton Rouge when he was fresh out of seminary. On every trip to see Maggie we made a point of participating in Sunday Eucharist at St. Mary's. We enjoyed reconnecting with Andy and thought he would be an ideal pastoral counselor for Maggie—just the kind of personality with whom she would mesh. We were also eager for Ellie, Paul, and Flynn to have the support the church and its sacraments give. We encouraged Ellie to go to St. Mary's when Maggie was able. Confirming our judgment, one of the St. Jude chaplains, independently of Nini and me, also recommended St. Mary's to them.

It was not only Andy who was the agent of Grace in Maggie's church experience, although both he and his associate rector the Rev. Laura Foster Gettys would play increasingly important roles in her life. But it was the gathered body of Christ in its action of eucharistic worship that made God present to Maggie's consciousness and encouraged her faith. The experience she describes is not uncommon: a beautiful place filled with symbols of faith reminding of the stories of God's action down through history, hymns of praise and thanksgiving, the presence of other persons whom one may know and admire, welcoming words from the persons there, the priest blessing in the name of God, perhaps some insightful words about the stories of faith, the enactment again of the crucifixion and resurrection in the sharing of bread and wine, a rush of tears, both joyous and sad, lifting a heavy load and bringing cleansing, release, and relief.

We do not decide to generate such experiences; they overtake us. We suffer them. Whatever psychological explanations may be proposed, such experiences come, we may believe, as gifts from God and as the experience of God's active presence. Maggie recalled the experience later in her summer recollections.

MCC, JUNE, 2011

I vividly remember the first time I walked into St. Mary's. It was hot outside, and my leg was in a brace at that point. I walked on two crutches, and I felt silly wearing my leg brace with my Sunday dress. Still, I had decided that I wanted to go to church, that as angry as I was at God for allowing me to have cancer, I needed to put forth some type of spiritual effort. Mama and I walked in through the front door and were greeted by a very nice stranger. He handed us the weekly bulletin and welcomed us to his church, a huge smile on his face. We sat down on a pew at the very back of the church. We were early, so the church wasn't full at all, but there were some gray-head ladies a few rows in front of us. One of them turned around and said hello to us. She must have noticed that I was on crutches because she asked me if I needed someone to bring the Eucharist to me. I smiled but said "No, thanks."

An organ began to play, and the music resounded off the church's high ceilings. I don't remember what I was thinking. I honestly don't remember thinking anything at all. In those moments, I was only feeling. There were no words or ideas in my mind, no logic or reason holding me back. I looked around me, at the people who were so kind and caring to a stranger, at the beautiful stained-glass windows and wooden pews, at the enormity of the church, the voices of the choir echoing around me, and I started to cry. I felt a wave of relief pass through me, a gush of emotions flooding from within me and out of my eyes. I was weeping, and I didn't know what I was weeping for, only that being in that church had facilitated it.

My mother reached out and put her arm around me, and I felt her tears on my shoulder. We eventually stopped crying enough to pay attention to the sermon and to this man who was Andy Andrews. I noticed from the way he spoke that he was deeply caring and immediately felt drawn to him. When it was time for Communion, I crutched to the front of the church, noticing the eyes of the congregation on me. Despite my futile attempts to hold back the tears, they came again, streaking my makeup across my face and drawing the stares of even more people.

Finally, I reached the front of the line, and I looked up at Andy. He smiled at me, and I felt like I owed him no explanation. Without hesitation or encouragement, he put his hand on my head and blessed me. I cried all the way to the back of the church. I do not know why the church and Andy triggered such a reaction from me. I only know that I was deeply moved.

And then, as we exited from the church, I saw her—the professor. Though I had already been taught by about eight wonderful teachers in my first year at Rhodes College, this professor was special. She was a religious studies professor, a woman I'd admired immensely and enjoyed as a teacher two semesters in a row. The year before, I'd spent hours in her office with her, asking and re-asking her to share her religious beliefs with me. I didn't know why it mattered to me when she was my teacher. After all, she was sharing many different views with us, approaching the subject from a scholarly, critical, and objective point of view, and playing "devil's advocate" on every possible occasion. What she actually believed should not have concerned me. Looking back, I think that I was so unsure of my own faith that I wanted validation. I wanted to hear the "secret" to faith from the woman who had all the answers. She refused, perhaps for this reason, to give me any answers, and I had concluded that she was an atheist.

I think on that day in St. Mary's I got an answer—or part of one. Though I cannot conclude exactly what she believes, I can conclude that something brought her to St. Mary's. Despite her brilliance, her multitude of prestigious degrees, and her ability to question everything, she still, for whatever reason, needed church. I found myself holding back tears as we made eye contact. She smiled mischievously, as if the secret was finally out. When she approached me, I asked if she came here often. "Not as much as I ought to," she said. Perhaps, then, she was not just a scholarly observer.

Maybe it was meant to be. Maybe it was just chance. I won't ever know, but I'm not sure it matters. The fact is, it happened.

I met with Andy many times after that day. I told him about my problems, my doubts about my faith, and my anger with God. He didn't have a cure for my anger. He didn't scold me or condemn me for anything, either. But he did assure me that my doubts and anger were understandable and even necessary parts of the long process of finding my own faith. In Andy, I found a confidante, a comfort, and a true testimony of real faith and experience.

EHH

Maggie's first experience at St. Mary's grew beyond that day in July. Andy became a source of strength and comfort as Maggie moved through the remaining long months of treatment and beyond. The experience opened Maggie more fully to the possibility of God and to an awareness of a broader, more pervasive sacramental presence of God in everyday life. It helped her to realize that Christian faith is not defined by narrow-minded and condemning "judgmentalism." Even if such a negative way of life is found in churches and in church people, there are also openness, acceptance, generosity of spirit—the caring of persons for one another.

The second of the two sacramental experiences also began in the early weeks of Maggie's treatment. Like the ongoing relationship that began with her first visit to St. Mary's, the friendship with Odie Harris continued to leaven her life of faith. In fact, the friendship with Odie, more than any other experience, pressed Maggie to ponder whether and what one can be thankful for if their cancer is not cured and their life is cut short. Is there a good that overrides even death? Odie helped Maggie to answer, "Yes."

Many of the young patients Maggie came to know at St. Jude became God's special "deputies of his weakness"[1] for her, but Odie's impact was greatest. We can look at Maggie's friendship with him in the light of Jesus's story of the sheep and the goats in Matthew 25. One of the surprising revelations of that story is that the needy ones, the hungry and the thirsty, the naked and the lonely, the sick and the imprisoned—in other words, those like Odie and Maggie—are themselves sacraments. If ministering to them is ministering to Christ, then they present Christ to the world. God acts in and through their weakness; they mediate the living presence of God. No doubt they do not think of themselves as places where God is making the divine Self present. They have not known it about themselves, even less have others known it about them. Yet it is a clear implication of the story: Christ is present in places where we do not expect to find a king or a lord, let alone the Lord of the Universe. The weak ones, therefore, are Christ's special deputies in weakness, unwitting agents of grace whose God-bearing role goes largely unnoticed, by themselves and by others. Sometimes, however, the encounter with a vulnerable and weak soul catches one up short; one is overcome with the experience of the Holy Presence. So it was for Maggie in her encounter with Odie. In the summer after St. Jude, she wrote about their first meeting, and the journal entries she wrote around the time of that meeting give a vivid sense of its impact on her.

1. Farrer, *Austin Farrer*, 210.

MCC, JUNE, 2011

The day I met Odie continues to stand out in my mind as a milestone of sorts, a day that changed a lot of things for me.

I was having one of those days that felt like it was from hell. I was nauseous, my leg was hurting, and I was terrified. Cancer was like that; some days felt like normalcy again, but others were as surprising and heart-wrenching as diagnosis. That day, I had woken up to hundreds of tiny brown hairs sprinkled across my white pillowcase, the last of the stubble that had clung to my scalp even though I'd shaved my head several weeks earlier. This time, the hair that fell from my head was out of my control. I felt powerless and a little sorry for myself. I dragged myself to the car, and my mother and I drove to the hospital and sat down in the waiting room, dreading the chemo that would come later that day. He sat across from me in a wheelchair, and he wore a hat.

Noticing him, I realized it was the first time all day I'd thought about anything or anyone other than myself. He looked sad. A few freckles sprawled about his pale skin, and I noticed that he, too, still had eyebrows, despite the lack of hair on his head. I was pretty sure he had once been a blonde, and I would later find out that I was right. He stared at the iPad in his lap while I stared at him.

Mama began to speak to the blonde lady who sat beside him. She looked even more afraid than we did. I joined in the conversation, and we traded the information that is customary in waiting rooms like these. Where are you from? When did you arrive here? What is your diagnosis? How is your treatment going? She told us about her son's disease, hepato-cellular carcinoma, a rare type of liver cancer that had infiltrated his lungs before they could catch it. She told us about the doctors at other hospitals who had taken one look at her little boy and concluded he had only weeks to live with no hope for cure. I was shocked that this had become a common conversation for her, even in front of her sick child. His name was Odie, and despite his young age of twelve, he had apparently been informed of the facts.

I looked across the waiting room and directly into Odie's big blue eyes expecting to see the most fear I'd ever seen before. But that is not what I saw. Instead, I saw something I was unable to name at the time, something I have come to identify as *strength*. I struck up a conversation with him. Why? It might have been because I pitied him, or because I wanted to change the topic of conversation to something a little lighter, but I think the biggest reason was that his strength called out to me. It was something I needed more of.

I saw him again only a few days later, at least I think it was only a few days later; it's hard to separate day from day, night from night when your life is a sea of hospital rooms. He was sitting in his wheelchair in solid tumor clinic, wearing that same black hat, staring down at his iPad. "What's up with you and that hat," I asked him, explaining my philosophy that baldness was nothing to be ashamed of or to cover up, especially in a room full of chemo patients. When I saw him later that day, he proudly smiled at me as he pointed at his hatless, bald head. We laughed together, and I gave him two thumbs up, feeling the warmth inside of me expand.

Another few days passed, and we saw his mother in the hallway. Without any warning, she embraced me, nearly knocking me off of my crutches. "I love you, Maggie," she said to me as she wept in my arms. "He's most like himself when he's with you."

It happened that we were both scheduled to begin our next sessions of chemotherapy on the same day. As Mama and my nurse wheeled me out of the elevator and down the hallway of the inpatient floor, another nurse called out to me. "Are you Maggie? He's been asking about you all day," she said as she pointed to a room with a patient in it. Sure enough, his name was written on the window. Odie and I, it seemed, had become friends. For the next few hours, I didn't sit around dreading the nausea that was to come as I received my IV fluids and pre-chemo medications. Instead, I breathed a little deeper. I closed my eyes and pictured the smile on a little boy's face, a smile that I had something to do with.

As the months went by and our friendship deepened, my tumor continued to respond to the cocktail of chemotherapy drugs I was receiving. But Odie's cancer did just the opposite. And as the months went by and our friendship deepened, I kept expecting some sign of fear to pop up in this little boy's beautiful blue eyes. Instead, I kept seeing only strength

MCC, FRIDAY, AUGUST 6, 2010.

When I went in for chemo last Wednesday, a pretty blonde woman rushed past the window and knocked on the door. It was Miss Laurie, Odie's mommy. I don't know if you remember who Odie is, but if you don't, he's the little boy of twelve who has liver and lung cancer and who I am madly in love with (in a non-creepy platonic way). Once, his mom told me that he acts most like himself when I'm around. We sit around being bald together in the waiting rooms and playing on our iPads. Anyway, his mother brightened my day.

Before that, Mama and I pulled into the parking lot for my chemo and I started vomiting because I thought too much about chemo (weird, huh? chemo is psychological). To my surprise, Odie was next door getting his chemo treatment still. I quickly begged my nurse to let me see him, and, because she was a beautiful person, like every other worker in this whole place, she wheeled me to his room and opened the door. There he was, bald and bedridden, pigging out on sour cream and Lay's onion chips. (It's always a great sign when chemo people are eating.) My heart starting reacting to the sight of him, and I wanted to take his place in that moment. I wanted to take his chemo for him. I wanted to take his tumors from him. I wanted him to be a normal, happy twelve-year-old boy who doesn't need a wheelchair or a hat or anti-nausea drugs or a feeding tube. We made small talk, and he seemed happy enough to see me. Then I had to wheel back to my room. But right as his door shut completely, the nurse outside his room said, "He's been asking about you all week."

Then I lost it. And all the nurses who hadn't heard probably wondered why tears were water-falling down my face. But if anyone had asked, I don't know what I would have told them because some things are too big and too terrible and too wonderful for words. And that's why I believe in God. Because whatever I feel when I look at that sweet, sweet kid is not just a product of brain chemistry (and believe me when I say I am an advocate of chemistry). Whatever I felt in that moment—in this moment, and in those moments that I will always hold close to me like delicate rose petals—whatever I felt is too big for explanation. And that is why I am okay with having cancer.

As another chemo draws near, I worry. I am scared of chemo. I'm not brave. I'm not a hero. I'm not strong. I'm a coward. A baby. A crier. But I have to do it. Because I'm not ready to give up. So here is what I'm going to think about: Odie. Odie and Alli and Carissa and Maribelle and Alleah and every little kid that is so much stronger than I and every bit as wise as I and way too mature because they got cancer. I'm going to suck it up and smile once a day and get up to pee every two hours like they want me to and be polite to the nurses who wake me up at 4 a.m. because these sweet little kids do it. And some of them don't have much of a chance of living afterwards. This is for them.

EHH

Maggie movingly describes the sacramental effect of meeting Odie. When she sees him, knowing that his prognosis is grim, she is overtaken by the desire to take his chemo in his place or to take his tumors away. Seeing him breaks her open and takes her outside herself. Whereas her main focus had previously been on her own cure, now Maggie's desire becomes Odie's healing. Now Maggie finds herself loving her neighbor, even "one of the least of these." Suddenly Maggie's focus is on loving rather than on being loved.

When one truly and rightly loves another, the love of the other becomes a non-grasping love of oneself. For truly loving another is desiring the good of the other. And if one's desire is for another's good, then the fulfillment of the other's good becomes the satisfaction of one's own desire and thereby a source of joy for oneself. When one rightly loves another, there can no longer be a conflict between loving oneself and loving another. Thus, God acts in Odie's weakness to give to Maggie what God demands of us all: that we love our neighbors as ourselves.

The meeting with Odie has another effect on Maggie. She has felt the doubt provoked by the power of natural science to explain events in terms of blind and purposeless natural causes. Could it be, she asks, that our beliefs and feelings are nothing more than a "product of brain chemistry?" But her encounter with Odie refutes the scientistic outlook. What she sees in him and what she feels for him are beyond words and "too big" for explanation. That they cannot be blithely tossed off as "brain chemistry" is for her a reason to believe in God. And, she says, somehow the experience even makes it okay that she has cancer.

Maggie fastens on strength as the quality that stands out in Odie's character. He was one of the weakest and most vulnerable of Maggie's friends at St. Jude, for he was dying. Yet in his weakness he was strong. He faced his cancer and accepted it. He was grateful for the life he enjoyed with his family and with his friends who loved him—including, especially including, Maggie. Pondering the strength she found in this weak one gives Maggie strength for herself. She will learn from Odie that it is possible to be thankful even in the face of impending death.

The sacramental experiences of the pre-surgery months of Maggie's treatment were by no means over and done. They would continue to leaven the life of her spirit and help her to become more aware of God's sacramental presence around her and of a value about life which suffering and death could not destroy.

Surgery was at last to be done on Thursday, September 2, 2010. She wrote on the Tuesday before that she was "madly excited." She would be getting a new metal tibia and a new metal knee. Even more important, she would be getting the entire tumor out. If all was well, the cancer would be completely dead.

As Maggie was to discover, however, chemotherapy does not always go according to plan and schedule. It is punctuated by surprises and disappointments.

The Hidden Kingdom

MCC, SUNDAY, SEPTEMBER 5, 2010

We've all felt it before: disappointment. In my old life, disappointment meant striking out at my softball games nearly every time I was up to bat. Disappointment meant drawing my letters backwards in four-year-old kindergarten and getting corrected. Disappointment meant missing a word when I was three and reading Amelia Bedelia books in a corner. And it meant going to bed early on Christmas Eve. When I got a little older, disappointment meant seeing the boy I had a crush on date someone else. Disappointment meant being curvier than most of the girls in my grade. Disappointment meant getting second place in the spelling bee. It meant getting glasses and braces at the same time. When I got even older than that, disappointment meant getting an A-minus on a paper. Disappointment meant losing a round of mock trial to another nationally ranked team. Disappointment meant having a faulty internet connection in my dorm room. It meant having too many places to be at the same time.

Then I got cancer and grew up. Disappointment became losing my life. It became giving up my passions for an entire year or more. It became fearing death. It became watching my friends on Facebook and wishing I could be with them. It became not being able to kiss my boyfriend because I don't have an immune system. It became separating my family between

Memphis and Brookhaven because of my disease. It became puking my guts out during chemo.

And perhaps the ultimate disappointment came on September 1 when I was told that my surgery was postponed because of my platelet count.

You might not understand why that was so bad for me, why it was nearly as horrifying as my diagnosis. But I'd been counting down the days for months. I'd been waiting for the day when I got rid of all the cancer inside of me. I'd been dreaming of getting my tumor out and of getting to finally put weight on my leg again. I'd been waiting for my turn to learn to walk again and see my friends again. I'd been waiting to see the light at the end of the tunnel, and it got snatched from me, without my consent. And whose fault was it? My own body's.

I know it's not logical for me to feel guilty about my platelets being low, but that's how I felt. Because it's my body, and I can't seem to control it. Because it turned on me.

Needless to say, I was depressed about the rescheduling of my surgery. And thanks to my chaplain's advice, I wallowed. I went to bed at about 5:00 p.m. and slept until noon the next day. I watched TV for hours and stayed inside all day. I ate lots of ice cream and watched many episodes of *Grey's Anatomy*.

There was only one person who could pull me out of my slump, and that was my mother. Maybe it's because she knows me best, and maybe it's because half of me is her. But the next day, we went to see a movie, and I had ice cream, an Icee, Sweet Tarts, and two Gibson's donuts in the same night. I wasn't eating my emotions. I was just eating because I could. And that night, we prayed for my platelets and meditated about them. And the next day, we found out that they were rising at a constant rate and will soon be up enough for surgery.

So the moral of the story is . . . I'm not sure this time. Disappointment is always bad, even when it's over an A-minus. But learning to overcome disappointment, to let go of the horrible feelings and guilt we sometimes feel, is important. Because no matter what happens, life goes on. And shouldn't we enjoy it?

EHH

As it turned out, the surgery was only delayed for four days. On September 6, when Maggie was just over three months into her eleven-month sojourn at St. Jude, the surgical team was able to go ahead. We knew immediately that the long procedure was successful in removing and replacing the targeted tibia and knee. That did not mean, however, that the most important objective had been reached. The tibia and knee were gone, but was all the cancer gone? It would be several long days of uneasy suspense before Maggie and Ellie would get this most important news.

MCC, TUESDAY SEPTEMBER 21, 2010

On Wednesday, September 15, 2010, my doctor and nurse practitioner walked into the hospital room I was in because of a post-surgery infection in my new leg. They sat down casually but with serious looks on their faces, and I sat up in bed, forcing a smile through my state of depression. Then Dr. Pappo spoke up. "We have the pathology report," he said.

The room started spinning. I couldn't hear, my vision blurred, and I started crying hysterically. "But you haven't even heard the results yet," you are probably thinking. That's what scared me so much; my life was about to change forever. There were two options: either the tumor had not responded well to chemotherapy or the tumor had responded well to chemotherapy. You see, I'd been waiting to know the answer to this question since May. And then I got it. I said, "How much is dead?" Then Dr. Pappo said, "100 percent." 100 percent is a lot. It's a whole. It's all of something and nothing of the other. In other words, all of my cancer was completely dead even before it was completely removed in surgery.

I know that moment should have been one of the best in my entire life. And though I did weep tears of joy, something was in the way of my moment of bliss. Just a day earlier, only a couple of days after I was sent home from the ICU, my leg was bright red and really swollen, and I had a high temperature at all times. So when my moment was here, I let it go, kind of like a bright red balloon inflated with helium and not tied down.

The non-tragic part of this story is that the news is still the same. My cancer is dead and gone. It won't come back.

And, now, finally, my infection is under control and I am back at Target House.

I have never been so thankful before: thankful for prayers and dreams, thankful for encouragement, thankful for modern medicine, and thankful for freedom from the hospital.

EHH

At the good news I could have proposed to continue our faith conversation. There were important questions that Maggie had raised but that I had not addressed. Nevertheless, it did not seem fitting to propose more abstract theological thinking. At this time such talk seemed neither here nor there, and I sensed that Maggie felt the same way.

All was well. There was good news to celebrate. There were thanks to be given. The cancer was dead, 100 percent dead, and removed from her body. She had a new leg and knee. These were the goals Maggie had focused on; now they were accomplished. It was only natural that she would expect the rest to be smooth sailing, a mopping up action of learning to walk with her new leg, completing the chemo protocol, getting home by Christmas, possibly even being back in school in January. It was not to be.

MCC, TUESDAY, OCTOBER 5, 2010

I was under the impression that after my surgery, everything would be easy and downhill. I thought that most of the pain was over. I thought that most of the hardship was over. I thought that most of the anguish and grieving of my cancer was over. But I thought wrong. People had tried to warn me. People had told me that my surgery would be extremely painful and that recovery would be the hardest thing I had been through yet, but I didn't believe them. What could be harder than chemotherapy? Right?

Needless to say, the surgery was hard. Not only did it put me in constant pain, but I was immobile and kept away from the public. I was attached to machines and required to carry around several contraptions connected to my body. And my new leg was three times the size of my other one. It is true that when I woke up from surgery my first things to say were "I did it!" and "two legs." But then I got quieter and more tired and found resting more appealing than any other activity. I lost my appetite, didn't like sunlight, and refused to write. It was one of my lowest times.

But time brought me out of the depression. I started wanting things again, things like food and cooking and my friends. Things like a peek into the organic chemistry book and a walk outside in the fall weather. And things like a meeting with my wonderful chaplain and a journal updating session.

So here I am, and I'm proud of myself. That's right. I said it. I'm proud of Maggie Cupit. I am proud of her, even though she has done zero school-work this semester. I am proud of her, even though she doesn't always drink her Ensure. I am proud of her, even though she cries easily right now. Because she fought cancer. She beat cancer. And now she's keeping it away. And the best part is: the worst part really is over.

EHH

But the worst part was not over. When she wrote the previous journal entry, Maggie could not have known that the remaining months at St. Jude would serve up as much suffering as it did. To have the greatest assurance of victory over the cancer, Maggie would have to undergo four more three-day and four more five-day rounds of chemotherapy. After the surgery the time between treatments grew longer and longer as it took longer for her body to recover and for her counts to come back to a level that would make treatment safe. There was no way the remaining treatments could be completed by Christmas. Further delays were necessary because of leg infections. One of these infections would require surgery and make Maggie have to learn to walk with her prosthetic leg and knee not once but twice. She would not go home until the beginning of May 2011, after almost eight more months at St. Jude. In addition to the slow process of physical recovery, Maggie would have to deal with the loss of fellow patients and with the frightening movement away from her safe place at St. Jude and back into the regular world: more pain, nausea, uncertainty, fear, grief, and doubt.

As Maggie struggled through the months between the surgery and Christmas, she was determined to take as positive an outlook as she could muster. In most respects, Maggie was a patient in the most basic sense of being the passive recipient of externally imposed treatments: chemotherapy, drugs to deal with leg infections, blood transfusions to boost her counts, and so on. But there was one part of her treatment that put Maggie in the agent's seat. Learning to walk on her new leg was something she could *do*, an action she could undertake.

MCC, SATURDAY, OCTOBER 23, 2010

Today I dressed in a cute outfit, wore makeup, and put on a cute pair of shoes . . . all for the first time in a long, long time. At the end of the day, or whenever I get back to my apartment, I usually sit down in my comfortable sweats or pjs and relax. But today, I sat down in my cute outfit and stayed in it . . . I'm actually still in it. I simply did not want to take it off.

Three days ago I was told that I was allowed to put weight on my leg for the first time in five months and bend my leg for the first time in over six weeks. Do you know what that's like? The first step I took, using my crutches of course, was so weird that it didn't feel like I was walking on my leg at all. It was kind of an "out of body experience," I think—though I've never been out of my body that I know of.

Since then, I've been walking and walking and walking, more than I'm required to at physical therapy, more than my mother makes me, and more than it takes to make my leg hurt. Because walking with two legs, all of a sudden—even if it is with crutches—after not getting to in so long, is a gift. And now walking isn't something I will ever do subconsciously or take for granted. I look forward to the day that I can walk without my crutches, but until then I'm enjoying walking with crutches.

The leg bending is a little bit different. The first day, I was told that I would start out by working my leg to fifteen degree bends at first, then thirty . . . and so on and so on. Day one, I bent my knee twenty-eight degrees. On day two, I bent it thirty-seven degrees, and on day three, I bent it fifty-eight degrees. Needless to say, I am an overachiever when it comes to physical therapy. I walk everywhere I go now, and refuse to bring the wheelchair with me.

My chemo has been delayed for weeks. I refuse to count because it upsets me so much. I can't control my counts and how quickly they rise. But I can control physical therapy. I can control my attitude. And I can control how much I use this leg.

EHH

Even as Maggie threw herself into physical therapy, she found her chemo treatments more and more brutal, harder and harder to endure. On top of that there was an infection in the long incision in her leg. Although she now accepted the fact that her treatment for Ewing's would not be finished by Christmas, Maggie was more than ready to be done with this stage of her life.

MCC, SATURDAY, OCTOBER 30, 2010

I finished my eighth chemotherapy session Thursday night. I spent yesterday rolling around the hospital trick or treating in my Halloween costume and wheelchair. And today . . . well, today should have been better than it was. There was a segment of the day that was good. My Grandpapa and Nini were in town, and Grandpapa brought some of his Rhodes friends to meet me. That was delightful. I loved talking to them and was really flattered to find that many of them keep up with my CaringBridge page. That part of my day was good.

But this morning, I woke up aching from the Vincristine and all the other chemicals I feed my body these days. I felt so achy that all I could really do was lie around. I slept most of the day away. And then I made a huge mistake. Instead of leaving the day the way it was, which was alright, I turned the day, or at least the end of the day, into a very bad day.

You might think that doing something as simple as picking up a laptop and looking at Facebook would be easy. It's not. Or at least it wasn't today. I don't want to get on Facebook only to see people who aren't me in pictures with my best friends. I don't want to sit here, a few blocks away from my college, while the entire world moves by without me. I'm even upset by the pictures of my best friends, smiling and having fun, making new friends and getting to know them. I should be happy for them. I should be happy for everyone I see on Facebook and in person, happy for them because they get to move on, happy for them that they are well, happy for them because they're normal teenagers living normal lives without cancer. But you know what? That's hard.

EHH

Nevertheless, even as Maggie continued to experience pain and feel deprived of her normal life, these months became a time of spiritual growth. She was recognizing and enjoying the good for which we are created. Maggie came to St. Jude already on a journey of faith, and her battle with cancer intensified it. Her journal shows that in fact she was living a faithful life and living it more intensely than she herself knew. Perhaps because the common understanding is that faith is believing things without reason or believing that God will grant all one's desires, she did not recognize that in the middle of her ordeal she was living a life of faith.

Maggie's more faithful life was not something our theological conversation had persuaded her into. Rather, faith was becoming more real and intentional because it was more a matter of experience, more a matter of heart and action than of belief and mind. The experience of St. Mary's and the friendship with Odie were alive and working within her spirit along with the experience of love and care which she had always known in her family but which were now being thrown into high relief. Reading her journal in the light of what we had said about faith in our email discussions, lets us see the sense in which Maggie's life was becoming faithful.

Maggie was not about to settle for a counterfeit faith. Her intellectual honesty in collision with the hard rocks would not allow it. She would not have a judgmental and condemning faith. She would not have a faith that sets itself in opposition to science and reason. She would not have a faith that thinks its own way of understanding is the only, the certain, the complete, the final truth. She would not use faith as a way of avoiding reality or as an attempt to manipulate God. She knew that belief in God would not guarantee delivery from cancer. If there were to be authentic faith in God, it would have to be a faith she could hold even if her cancer were not cured. It must be a faith that promises ultimate good, a good that is good whether one lives or dies, a good that is good no matter what. Such a good, I had urged in our faith exchange, is the good God intends us to have, the good for which we are created. Authentic faith in God, therefore, means consenting to receive the good God intends even if it means undergoing radical change and accepting suffering while being thankful in the midst of it.

In the faith discussion, we proposed that the ultimate good and the good for which God creates us is that we become persons who love God with our all our heart, soul, mind, and strength and our neighbors as ourselves. Being such a person living among such persons is good no matter what the accidental conditions and circumstances of life may be. This good is the one intrinsic and eternal good. It is the-good-no-matter-what.

Maggie needed to experience this good and to know it as a good that even innocent young patients facing death can have. She needed to experience this good, not just to think speculatively about its possibility. How likely could it be that in the middle of continued suffering, Maggie would be given this experience? Yet, it may well be that it is only in the midst of suffering that the good of loving and being loved can truly be known to be the-good-no-matter-what.

One could not possibly enjoy this good by oneself. By its very nature it requires participation in a community of persons. Receiving the good for which God created us is the same thing, therefore, as becoming part of a community of reciprocal loving, part of the kingdom of heaven, and part, therefore, of the very life of God.

This understanding of the good God intends for us follows from the understanding of God as the eternal and perfect act of self-giving love. So understood, God is a perfect community of perfect love, eternally enacted and eternally fulfilled within God's own life. The Christian idea of God as Trinity of persons in unity of being expresses this understanding. The ultimate good that God desires for us is to share in God's own life of perfect reciprocal loving by loving God with all our being and our neighbors as ourselves.

Now we participate in that life only partially, fitfully, incompletely. Our experience is that we fall far short of being persons who love God and our neighbors. Do we not always speak truth when we confess in the words of the *Book of Common Prayer*, "We have not loved you [God] with our whole heart; we have not loved our neighbors as ourselves"?[1] But it is the Christian hope that God will act to complete and perfect this good in us, this good for which we feel ourselves to be made, this good which, when fully realized, would be our perfection. Therefore, from this idea we imagine its perfect fulfillment. It would be the perfected kingdom of God or kingdom of heaven, a community in which each member actually does perfectly love both God and neighbor.

This Christian hope has yet to be realized, but to the extent that persons manage sometimes to love their neighbors as themselves, so that they are made happy by seeing God's good for their neighbors fulfilled, to that extent the kingdom is already present. The kingdom of heaven, Jesus said, is like a "treasure hidden in a field" (Matt 13:44), or like "leaven" hidden in dough (Matt 13:33). It is present but hidden in the actions and relationships of persons.

It is hidden in two ways. First, it is hidden in the actions of particular persons in their particular actions of genuine love. When we observed that Maggie's experience at St. Mary's and her friendship with Odie Harris were sacramental, we were recognizing that the kingdom of heaven was hidden

---

1. *Book of Common Prayer*, 360.

in the quite familiar and ordinary actions of persons and their interactions with each other. The experiences were "sacramental" for Maggie because God's action in Maggie's life was given to her through them.

But the kingdom of heaven is hidden in another sense. It is hidden "by" the world. God's presence in human actions is made harder to discern because of the "slings and arrows of outrageous fortune" and especially because human efforts at loving God and their neighbors are all mixed up with fear, jealousy, pride, anger, lust, and so on—not to mention preferences for private and temporary goods. Human motives are not clean and singular but complex and confused. Consequently, the element of genuine love in them can be hard to find. But there are circumstances in which true love in the sense of desiring the other's real good is purified and made to stand out. So it was for Maggie in her life as a cancer patient. She had first recognized it at the beginning of her year of treatment when she "saw a little bit of God" in the friends sitting in her Target House room. Now the experience deepens and spreads.

What I describe abstractly, Maggie experienced concretely. She knows the good God desires for us by experiencing it directly and living it intentionally. Going through pain and facing the possibility of early death, she finds herself being loved and loving. She knows that God is in the loving. She finds herself, whether or not she knows it in these terms, a participant in God's kingdom, though the kingdom is as yet imperfect and partial.

The kingdom is so partial and imperfect that we are scarcely aware of its existence. But once we do sense that the-good-no-matter-what is present, we may choose to commit to its growth. To commit to it means cooperating with the grace that is given by being willing to be changed and even to suffer for it.

The acid test of commitment to the good for which God has created us is gratitude or thankfulness. No matter what change and suffering must be endured in order to be part of the eternal act of love that God is, gratitude should reverberate as the great bass note underlying the life committed to it. In the words of the *Book of Common Prayer*, "It is right, and a good and joyful thing always and everywhere to give thanks to you, Father Almighty, Creator of heaven and earth."[2] "Always and everywhere." The words are unconditional.

We might say that Maggie wakes up to find herself already living a life of faith in the kingdom of heaven. Not that she thinks about her experience

2. Ibid., 361.

in those terms or in terms of the creeds or of explicitly Christian theology. She does not. But she is quite conscious of knowing for herself and others a good that death does not destroy. She knows that living within a community of reciprocal loving is good within itself, that it is good no matter what. From the perspective of Christian understanding, this is the good God desires for us, for which we must be willing to be changed and to suffer, and because of which our stance in life should be one of gratitude.

Life in the kingdom of heaven was not something wholly new to Maggie. She had always known she was part of a family where she cared for the others and the others cared for her. She also had friends among whom there was genuine caring each for the other. What is new for Maggie is the degree to which she becomes aware of the reciprocity of love and the consequence that one's happiness is all bound up with the happiness of others. She knows that the actions, words, and presence of others around her mean that they desire her healing and will receive joy from it. At the same time she knows in her own emotions and actions toward them that she desires their well-being and will receive joy from its fulfillment. In the heightened consciousness of reciprocal love, Maggie knows it as something perfect and somehow timeless. These are the qualities that the good God desires for us must surely have. And surely the nurture and extension of reciprocal loving makes it worth suffering for.

It is the battle with cancer that brings Maggie to early wisdom about these matters and to an intentional commitment to life in the kingdom, knowing that the kingdom's reciprocal loving is the-good-no-matter-what, the good God desires for us, and a good that in a mysterious way is beyond the passing of time. Even cut short, such a life is forever good.

MCC, THURSDAY, SEPTEMBER 30, 2010

Why did this cancer happen? At night I close my eyes and remember the richest things of my life so far—friendship and laughter and family and that time I climbed a mountain with the pages in Shenandoah Valley. Sometimes I start to cry. Other times I smile a huge smile. Other times I laugh out loud and my mother asks me what's so funny. I remember mock trial trips and performances, inside jokes with the team, and the time I had a huge crush and online stalked a guy from the UCLA mock trial team. I remember sorority meetings and events and formals and my best Chi Omega sisters. I remember the times I cooked and watched movies in the common room of my dorm and had at least ten people sitting next to me. I remember running down the halls with Sheerin and disturbing people and Allie yelling out "Quiet hours!" It was a weeknight, but we just laughed louder. I remember my teachers and how much I learned and how much I miss my old life. And I know that I wouldn't change a single thing about my life so far at all—except for those times I spent worrying and punishing myself for not being perfect.

My life was so good that I think I finally understand why people always seem ready to die when it's their time (not that it's my time yet). When you have time to look back on your life, and I mean really look back and spend hours doing nothing but remembering every day because there is nothing better to do, you get this feeling. And you know that you did it right, your life I mean. You know that it was full of life. It was full of love. It was just full, period. And somehow, even if there isn't an afterlife and you're about to lose consciousness, you know that your memories are enough. Because you lived them, and when you close your eyes you can taste them, like the aftertaste of hot chocolate. And they can never disappear because they happened, and they are now forever sealed in time. And no one can take them from you or from time. That's how I feel when I think of my life so far.

Some days I wish I could fast forward time or skip this chapter of my life. But maybe I'm a little glad that I am living each day right now with cancer slowly and in the moment, because that's the way people learn things—life changing things like this. I pray that whoever controls the universe knows how thankful I am for this moment and all the wonderful ones I have had leading up to it.

EHH

In the months after surgery while Maggie is learning to walk on her new leg and discovering that there is still much to endure, she becomes ever more aware of the love she is receiving. It comes from different sources. One important source is the physicians, nurses, and therapists at St. Jude. Reflecting on her experience with them she writes in her journal that they have become a big part of her life. It is not unusual to speak of persons as part of one's life. But there are many ways persons can be "part" of one's life, and they are not all instances of the hidden presence of the kingdom of heaven. Maggie knows that these caregivers' part in her life is the effect of their desire for her well-being: they "really do care about me. And

I really depend on them," she says. And she recognizes in them what she had felt when she met Odie. As she desired his good, to take his tumors away, to undergo his treatment for him, so they desired her healing. She understands their way of being toward her, and she hopes that she herself will be able to live that way toward others. There is nothing unusual about Maggie's experience here. It is a common experience to which we pay too little attention. Maggie was waking up to it.

MCC, WEDNESDAY, OCTOBER 6, 2010

Today, more than usual, I noticed how deeply involved I am with the people who work at my hospital. It all started in rehab. I started to cry when I remembered that my physical therapist, Christina, is leaving in December because she is just a student right now and has to go home to graduate. We also had the famous St. Jude teen art show today. It was quite the event, and all of our paintings (the teen patients) were covered with black paper. When it was our turn in the show, we got to rip the black paper off the paintings. I didn't expect anyone to come. My painting was just something I did for fun, but my favorite nurse Julie showed up just to watch. Then my chaplain Lisa, another one of my favorite people, showed up to watch the show. After spending time with her, I ran into my friend Beth, who is really Dr. Stuart, a fellow at St. Jude. She feels like one of my best girlfriends these days. She's so loving, and we talk about random things. She always tries to visit me when possible. Also, my nurse practitioner Patti sent me a text saying she loved my artwork.

It really wasn't until I starting thinking later that I realized how big a part of my life all of those people have become. I take this for granted a lot—this time I mean. After all, I am getting chemo and fighting cancer and whatnot. Most people wouldn't exactly envy my position. But when I'm done and move on from here, I know there will be a part of me that is heartbroken, because all the people who spend my days with me really do care about me. And I really depend on them. I hope that, when I grow up, I am lucky enough to have a job in which I affect people like that. I hope that I am lucky enough to love my job as much as the people at St. Jude do, too.

And maybe while I'm still here, I can focus on enjoying this time because of the people who care for me here.

EHH

Maggie also discovers during these fall and winter months that the hidden kingdom extends beyond the closed circle of persons she knows and lives with into a world of persons she will never know and who also desire the well-being of persons they will never know. These anonymous persons choose to bind up some of their joy in acting for the good of unknown cancer patients. These persons include those who give money, who come to St. Jude to teach knitting or Japanese or guitar, celebrities who come to entertain, and those who participate in fundraising walks or runs. Given the strife that is so prominent a part of the human world, it is important to recognize that the hidden kingdom extends through and can be found in more of the world than we might at first think. Maggie discovers that it does.

MCC, SATURDAY, DECEMBER 4, 2010

Have you ever had one of those moments where you imagine your future self, thinking back to the present time, but as a memory? You're doing something that you know is completely worthwhile, and there is nowhere else you'd rather be and no one else you'd rather be with. You're there, in that future memory, smiling and laughing and wishing you could make the moment last longer than it ever will. And even though you know that's impossible, that this moment will fade away and lose a little of itself, piece by piece, you imagine, just for a moment, that this moment is timeless. You imagine that this moment is actually not a moment, but a photograph, and that it will never lose its detail or color or luster. I had one of those moments today.

It was more like a couple of hours, and they were spent outside Target House, lining the street with my mom and little sister and my physical therapist Christina, who has come to be one of my best friends. I in my wheelchair and my mother in her cap (just kidding; that was a reference to "The Night Before Christmas"). But really, I was in my wheelchair, and Mama was in her coat, and so were all of us. And we were lining the streets because the St. Jude marathon was going on.

It was rumored that this year, there were over 6,500 runners. And we sat there cheering and shouting and clapping because they were all running for us. They were all running for me. And for one of the first times, I realized that I'm not the only one fighting my cancer. I've known that my family and friends have been behind me. Don't get me wrong. But for the first time, the people who make St. Jude possible, the people who donate to St. Jude, had faces. And they were all running past me. Strangers kept pointing at me and yelling, "This is for you!" And my physical therapist, Christina, who is leaving next week to go home and graduate, was standing beside me, smiling and laughing.

I just wanted to press pause because things seemed a little bit perfect. I looked up and saw tears running down my face and the face of Miss Becky, another patient's mom. I started to cry, but I cleared the tears away because I wanted to spend time laughing and smiling with Christina instead. I saw six girls from my school run by wearing "Team Maggie May" t-shirts. I don't know how else to explain it but to say that I was filled with an overwhelming sense of joy and gratitude. The people who ran did that for me and all the kids who are like me. I hope that, one day, I can do something to fight cancer as well. I guarantee it won't be running, but I hope it will be even more powerful.

EHH

Notice two things in the previous journal entry: the sense of joy and gratitude and the sense of timelessness and perfection. Here Maggie seems to say that the very fact of other people trying to help her and others beat cancer is something perfect and timeless. Perfection and timelessness are qualities of divine life. Maggie senses that running to raise money for cancer fighting is a good that stands out from conditional goods, which last only for a time. It is a good beyond time because it is done for the good of the cancer patients, such that the runners will receive joy in the realization of good for those patients. The joy of the runners is tied to good for the patients. Seeing this, Maggie is filled with "an overwhelming sense of joy and gratitude." This plain ordinary event of running a race on a Saturday in Memphis hides within itself the presence and the activity of the kingdom of heaven. It is sacramental.

Maggie's experience of the hidden kingdom, however, was strongest with her family and in her friendship with Odie.

MCC, SUNDAY, OCTOBER 17, 2010

One of the biggest things that I've learned lately, or perhaps rediscovered lately, and something that I noticed on both of my outings was this: I love spending time with my family. I love hanging out with Flynn and Mama, whether we are watching a movie we picked out on Netflix or just sitting around together in the hospital waiting rooms as we wait to be called for an appointment. I love knowing that whenever something hurts—my body or my feelings—Flynn and Mama will be the first ones to help me feel better. And they will love doing it. Whenever we get home after a long day, I can't wait to get comfortable on the couch and snuggle with Flynn or get a foot rub from Mama. And I hope it doesn't sound like I like being around them because they are my servants. It's just that I know how much they care about me, and I care about them, too. When I go to bed at night, they are the ones that I pray for the most. They are the ones that I can't wait to see when I wake up in the morning. And in the morning, they are the reason I am able to crawl out of bed. Every time I start to cry at the hospital because I am afraid or upset, they don't get frustrated with me. They don't tell me to stop being so sensitive or get over it. They don't tell me to calm down or stop being so selfish. Instead, Flynn pats my back and tells me that it's okay, and Mama hugs me or talks to me about why I'm upset. And what they do to make me feel better is just what I need. It never fails. They do the perfect things. Maybe it's because they know me better than anyone else.

MCC, WEDNESDAY, NOVEMBER 3, 2010

I have always loved my family. I have always loved spending time with them. And they have always been the ones who have comforted me most. But having cancer and going through this experience has allowed me to spend a lot more time with my Mama and Flynn than I would have spent otherwise, and all of this time has reminded me how much I love them and how much I need time with them.

I think when you turn into a teenager you really start depending on your friends—in some ways even more than you depend on your family. And then you turn into a grownup. And most people never get to experience again that complete dependency on their parents that they felt when they were children. But when something like cancer happens, and your world is flipped upside down and nothing makes sense anymore and all you have left with you in the universe is your family, you become completely dependent on that family. And that's how I've become. And because of that, my love for my family has grown even more, which I didn't know was possible.

You know when you're a little kid and you absolutely adore you mother? In fact you idolize her some times. You want her around all the time. You cry when she leaves, and slumber parties scare you because your mom won't be there. At least that's how I was. Anyway, that seems to fade as you grow and gain your independence. But I guess what I'm ultimately trying to say is that that's the way I feel again. And I'm very grateful that I've been given the opportunity to feel that way again. My mother is my hero. If only I could be that brave, that faithful, that full of love all the time.

Finally, I want to leave you with something special, something I didn't want to share at first because it's mine. It's important for me to have a "safe place" to escape to in my imagination whenever things are especially painful here. For example, when my port is accessed, a one inch needle is stuck into my chest, so I close my eyes and think of my safe place, my corner of the universe. I figure that if it's a perfect place for me it may make you feel good too. Here it is:

When I was much younger, my grandmother Anne, used to live in a house on Perkins Drive in Brookhaven. It was a small house, with two bedrooms and two bathrooms. My safe place is in the den and kitchen area. A huge fireplace with freshly chopped wood sits in the middle of the den, sending out tiny sparks, lots of warmth, and the smell of a really good fire. A big blue wrap-around couch lies along the other wall, holding memories of Sissy and me moving the cushions around and making pretend dog cages for ourselves. A wooden rocking chair sits in the corner, one of those old reassuring pieces of furniture, where I saw my baby sister get rocked. On the left is the kitchen island with a few barstools for seating. That's where Sissy and I liked to sit. And the meal being prepared in the kitchen is Anne's specialty: spaghetti. My safe place smells like spaghetti and fire. It's warm in there, and it's full of memories that I treasure. But most of all, it's full of love.

EHH

While Maggie was reflecting in her journal and coming through it to a greater awareness of her life in the hidden kingdom, she was pulled up short. The Saturday before Thanksgiving she had a difficult chemo treatment, and the knowledge that she still had six more to go made it worse. And on the following Monday, there was an event that would have thrown her into near despair had it occurred before the spiritual growth she had been receiving. Instead, Maggie's focus on the-good-no-matter-what enabled her to maintain a spirit of gratitude.

MCC, MONDAY, NOVEMBER 20, 2010

Dear God, whatever you are, wherever you are,
    Thank you. Thank you for science. Thank you for second chances.
    Thank you for the people who take care of me.
    And thank you for chemotherapy.

MCC, WEDNESDAY, NOVEMBER 22, 2010

I went in for a checkup this morning. I had a few expectations for today, simply because my entire family is here to celebrate Thanksgiving with me. Since I can't go home, they came to me.

But when we got into the clinic and my nurse practitioner walked in the door we knew something was wrong . . . because she took one look at my scab, opened up her pretty eyes really big, and said, "I'll be right back." Patti came back to the room with Dr. Pappo, and they both examined my scab a little more closely. Keep in mind, this is no regular scab. This is the semi-healed incision which was made in replacing my leg with metal. So Dr. Pappo looked really worried too and said, "We better call Lunetha." Lunetha is the wound care specialist at St. Jude, a pretty, energetic woman with a tiny body and a huge heart. Lunetha came into the room several minutes later, and we all felt much better because she reassured us that this infection was superficial, and I was going to be fine. And I was fine.

But the story doesn't end there. Lunetha then proceeded to pull off my entire, foot-long scab, swab out all of the puss that was underneath, and cut (yes cut as in with scissors) the top layer of tissue out of my incision. I was given no sedatives or numbing medicines until after all of the cutting was done. So basically, one could say that I had surgery while I was awake. And I barely cried. Take that, cancer. Not only did this happen, but I was informed that I have lost over 20 pounds since I got to St. Jude in May, and I have to start taking a pill to stimulate my appetite.

So now I'm sitting in the bed resting up for my Thanksgiving dinner tonight with the family and, to my surprise, I'm finding my situation nothing to fret about. And this is progress, because a few days ago, all I could do was feel sorry for myself. And that was before the new leg ordeal and the weight problem.

It doesn't make a lot of sense, but this Thanksgiving is in the midst of the worst thing I've ever had to go through, and yet I feel I have the most to be thankful for. A book I was reading told me to make a little list of twenty things that I'm grateful for, and I almost hesitate to post this because it seems so cliche around Thanksgiving, but I'm going to write it anyway.

1. my family
2. my best friends (you know who you are :))
3. chemotherapy, but not its side effects
4. Dr. Pappo, Patti, and Julie
5. Odie
6. squirrels, owls, elephants, and all other animals
7. civil rights
8. animal rights (though there should be more)
9. oak trees and acorns
10. warm blankets
11. St. Jude Children's Research Hospital
12. my recent rise to fame
13. memories
14. Rhodes College
15. chemistry
16. music
17. my mock trial team
18. femininity
19. the ocean
20. my grandmother's spaghetti

EHH

The following Christmas Day entry strikingly expresses Maggie's experience that loving and being loved are the root of joy and thankfulness and
are in fact the good-no-matter-what, the good which death cannot destroy.
She goes on to say that the joy, the goodness lived in the moment, was so
good and so meaningful that it "almost" did not matter about there being
an afterlife. I believe Maggie's experience here is that we are created to love,
that we can only be fulfilled by loving, and that the loving in which we
will be fulfilled calls for a life beyond death. This experience, by no means
peculiar to Maggie, may be the most rational source, other than the resurrection, of the Christian belief in the life to come. If we believe in the God
who creates out of love, then there is good reason also to believe that God
will not frustrate the very purpose for which we are created and the hope
God has placed at the center of our being.

MCC, SATURDAY, DECEMBER 25, 2010

I'll be honest: I had my doubts. I had just started a new medicine, an in-
sanely strong antiviral that gave me constant nausea and stomach pains. I
had just been through eleven grueling rounds of chemotherapy and three
intensely emotional goodbyes. I had a metal leg for the first time on Christmas, and all I wanted was to be well, go back to school, and get control of
my life. But, even though a big piece of my heart ached for Odie, I did more
than just get through the day. As the snowflakes began to fall early in the
morning at 8:00 a.m., I watched the most perfect Christmas I'd ever had
unfold.

Sissy, Flynn, and I slept in the same room, as we did on every Christmas Eve, and, as she did on every Christmas morning, Flynn pulled us
out of bed way earlier than we would have liked. We went through our
stockings while we waited for Anne to come over from her hotel, and, one
gift at a time, we got to the bottom of the pile. Some homemade and many
special ordered, they all came from the heart. I got everything I asked for.
But the joy that I felt came from having all of my family with me or on the
way—and being alive.

It's hard to explain what I mean by that unless you've ever seen your
life flash before your eyes. I know that we all have moments of gratitude and
appreciation for life, but, sadly, I don't think everyone fully comprehends

what meaning life has until it is nearly taken away. It's almost as though, if you understood how meaningful life was, you wouldn't worry about there being an afterlife. This life would be almost enough. I say "almost" because I don't think I could live if I didn't hope for some type of heaven. There are too many people that I love too much to say goodbye to forever. And if I'm ignorant for believing in something besides this world, then let me be ignorant.

So this year was special. The first time I heard the words "there's a chance you have cancer," I panicked. If you know me, then melodramatic probably comes to mind when you think of me. This situation definitely fit that description. I didn't know if I would have another month to live, another year to live, or another Christmas to live. And slowly, treatment by treatment and month by month, I learned a little about living in the moment. So, today, I blocked out the future and forgot about the past (except for the good memories), and spent a perfect day with my perfect family. I ate way too much junk food and told a few jokes that no one laughed at but me. I wore a hat that looks like a squirrel and let my big sister give me a makeover. I caught some snow in my mouth and stood up and screamed in a movie theater as I watched myself on the big screen for the first time. I soaked up life and showed off my new ability to walk. And before I knew it, the day was gone and I was wishing it wasn't. My Christmas was so good I forgot I had cancer . . . and that's pretty darn good.

And the best part? It's not over yet. Merry Christmas.

Figure 1: Before treatment: Maggie with her mother Ellie: May, 2010

Figure 2: Treatments begin: June, 2010

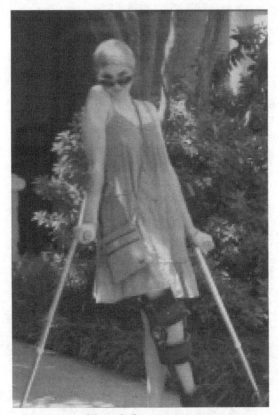

Figure 3: Confidence before surgery: summer, 2010

Figure 4: Maggie with NP Patti Peas and Dr. Alberto Pappo: summer, 2010

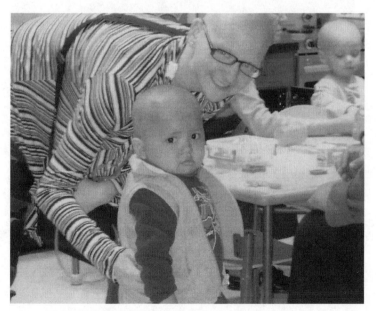

Figure 5: Battling cancer with Baby Kya: late summer, 2010

Figure 6: Halloween at St. Jude: NP Patti Peas, Maggie, Dr. Beth Stewart

Figure 7: Visitors from Baton Rouge: Grandpapa, Maggie, Nini, Flynn: autumn, 2010

Figure 8: Best Christmas ever: Anne Houston (Sissy), Maggie, Flynn, grandmother
Anne

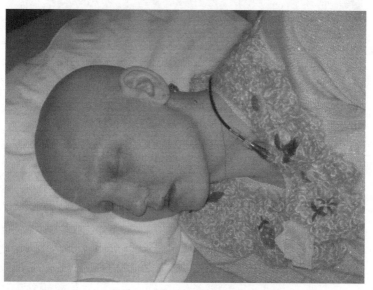

Figure 9: A terrible treatment after Christmas: January, 2011

Figure 10: Odie Comforts Maggie

Figure 11: Maggie, Carissa, Odie, Flynn, and Rachel before the Prom: April, 2011

Figure 12: Annual St. Jude Marathon, December, 2011: Anne, Anne Houston, Flynn, Maggie, Ellie, Paul

Figure 13: Rhodes College Graduation: Anne Houston, Ellie, Anne, Maggie, Flynn: May, 2014

Figure 14: Celebrating Graduation with her St. Jude Team: NP Patti Peas, Dr. Alberto Pappo, chaplain Lisa Anderson, NP Valerie Pappo, Maggie, Dr. Beth Stewart, Dr. Liza Johnson, RN Julie Morganelli: May, 2014

8

Choosing Life, Staying the Course

EHH

Christmas Day, 2010 concluded the first eight months of Maggie's twelve months at St. Jude with a strong experience of the good for which we are created. Things were looking good all around. The cancer was dead and gone from her body, and her hard work at physical therapy had her walking well with her new leg. There were, she thought, only four more treatments to endure. She could now look forward to taking up her research internship at St. Jude in the coming summer and returning to college life at Rhodes in the fall. The end of her ordeal was in sight.

Then came the first treatment of the New Year, the one after which she would have only three to go. It was awful, so bad she said she could not take any more. On top of that awful treatment, just a few days later, she and her mother discovered that they had miscounted. Instead of three there were four treatments to go. Anticipating that the others would be as awful as the one just completed, Maggie was distraught. She now saw death as something to be desired.

Knowing that discontinuing the treatments would likely lead to death, she told her mother and Dr. Pappo she wanted to stop. Ellie gave her the choice.

Maggie chose life, and the choice as she describes it was an act of the faith she was now living.

MCC, WEDNESDAY, JANUARY 5, 2010

What I remember of this last chemo treatment, though the memory is quickly fading, is that it was simply awful. When I left the hospital Sunday afternoon, I recall spitting out words like "I'm never going back," "You can't make me," and, "I'm done." And I was very serious.

I vomited constantly, more than usual even. I didn't sleep much at all. The anti-nausea drugs, which usually just helped me to sleep, had worn off; my body was just too used to them at that point. I was taking maximum doses of every drug I could take for nausea, and we'd even tried Marinol, a legal drug made from the marijuana plant. Nothing worked. My throat was raw from all the dry heaving I'd done the last five days. My whole body smelled like chemo. I didn't understand how some people, little kids especially, could be relatively unfazed by chemo's side effects. It made me feel extremely jealous of them. I also kept reminding myself that I could have been done with chemo at that point, if only I hadn't had all of the setbacks due to my "tired" bone marrow. I think I had cried for the entirety of that chemotherapy treatment, begging the doctors and nurses and whoever came into the hospital room to let me leave. I just felt like I couldn't do it anymore.

MCC, WEDNESDAY, JANUARY 12, 2011

A couple of days ago my mom found my old chemo schedule. At the bottom of the sheet, there were four chemo sessions, two five-day and two two-day treatments. This had to be a mistake, I thought. So when we got to clinic yesterday we asked for another schedule. And now we know that I have four chemos left, not three. And two are those terrible, awful, five-day ones.

I felt like I couldn't breathe, like the world was ending, and everything started to go dark. I felt like everyone was staring at me, pushing me forward into more and more chemo, the chemo that destroys my body and takes away my memory. The chemo that makes me someone I have never seen before. I still feel like that. I feel like just breathing is too hard and that everyone was counting on me and I let them down. I feel like the room is spinning and nothing I do is good enough. I feel like my blankey is of absolutely no comfort and my friends are too far away to help. I feel like people won't stop talking about me, no matter what I do. I am lost and alone and afraid and incredibly irritable.

It's all my fault, because it's my body and I'm the one that got cancer. What did I do wrong? I feel like there is nothing to look forward to because I'm not me anymore and I have to start from scratch. Everything I worked for has blown away in the wind, and I am left alone, naked, for people to laugh at and ridicule. I am an ugly duckling, and I will never turn into a swan. I am a frog who has no hope of becoming a prince. I limp when I walk. I cannot run, and skipping is not even in the picture. I am tense, and my shoulders hurt from carrying the weight of my head. I am not human anymore.

I need a time out. I need the voices in my head to stop making noise. I need understanding. I know that I have my family with me, always by my side, here to help. But they can't take away one of the chemos, one I thought wasn't there. A big, bad wolf. An evil witch. My worst nightmare. All combined but way, way worse. And no matter how much people try to understand, they can't. No matter how much people want to take my pain away, they can't.

I'm sorry if this journal lacks words of wisdom or inspiration, but I'm not very wise right now. I'm just trying to get through the day.

Perhaps the most astounding part of this situation is the universe's ability to propel me backwards in time, or to stop time altogether. So I sit in my room day after day watching the clock tick slower and slower and watching my friends go home, die, and disappear. My time is frozen, and yours is not. So I ask myself questions like, "Why me?" and, "What did I do to deserve this?" I remind myself that a thing called *karma* exists and that "what goes around comes around," whatever that means. To what end? Why does it matter in the grand scheme of things? What is the grand scheme of things, anyway?

I thought I only had three chemotherapy treatments left. I thought that I had two short ones and a long one. And today they told me that I had four left. I immediately broke down, losing every ounce of hope that I had managed to muster up out of ashes and dust. It was like getting a failing grade on a paper that I had worked my butt off on, but worse. If this were myself of a year ago, I'd be at school, holed up in the library with a chai latte, worrying about which boy to ask to formal and which girlfriend to spend the evening with. My biggest fears would consist of obesity, natural disasters, and heartbreak.

I laugh at the girl who sat in my place last year. I laugh at my friends who think they know what I feel but fail miserably. I own nothing but the clothes on my back and the food in my stomach. They make me gain weight here. They threaten me with feeding tubes and TPN, a substance with total nutrition that goes through the port and directly into the bloodstream. They make me stuff myself until I feel like I am about to enter a coma. And what do I get in return? Chemotherapy, of course, and lots of it.

I resent this whole situation I have been thrown into. I resent the universe for allowing so many innocent children to suffer so much. I resent the universe for allowing me to be a part of such terror. Perhaps this is how victims of the holocaust felt—abandoned, forgotten, terrified—because death isn't really supposed to be something to look forward to, or at least it never was before I had cancer.

So I told my mother I couldn't do it anymore. I told her I was finished. Mama could have reacted in any way. She could have gotten angry. She could have tried to talk some sense into me. She could have told me the truth: that without chemo, I would probably die. But she just looked at me, saw the pain that I was in, the pain that I had been in for the past year, and she nodded. I'm not saying that my mother was alright with my decision to end treatment. She probably knew that the drugs were talking and not me. She probably knew that I would come around. But in that moment, I finally felt like I had a choice. I felt like I was in control of my destiny, in control of my treatment. I felt like I had the right to decide whether or not I could continue

MCC, SATURDAY, JANUARY 15, 2011

After a few days of recovery—days full of breathlessness, weight loss, aching, and fatigue, to name just a few of the side effects—I altered my plan. I told Dr. Pappo, Patti, and Mama that I was ready to go ahead with my chemo. And I was hoping that my counts would recover quickly so that I could go into the next treatment right away.

I like to think that chemotherapy and fighting this disease are choices that I made, that if I had decided to succumb to my disease I could have, that if I wanted to I could have called off this whole thing. Whether or not I am any authority in this at all may not even be worth discussing. What I do know, however, is that today was better than yesterday. I was less nauseous, the tiniest bit more energetic, a whole lot more talkative, and able to bend my leg in physical therapy over 105 degrees, even before stretching. After talking to my psychologist, I am confident that the next chemo, which is only twenty-four hours long, will be easier. That, my friends, is way more than I could have begun to admit yesterday.

I think there were a couple things that gave me the desire to keep fighting and to keep living. The first thing was my mother. I firmly believe that she went through just as much as I did during that time. Sure, she didn't have all the physical torment of chemo, but she had to watch me go through it. She had to sit beside me, day in and day out, and listen to me cry and complain and, in my delirium, tell her to tell my sisters goodbye for me. She had to watch me revert to childhood and cry out for her in the hardest moments. She had to watch my heart break as I watched my classmates continue with their normal lives while I waited for my life to begin again. She felt every ounce of misery I felt that year. And yet, she loved me and knew me enough to trust me with a decision as vital as whether or not to continue chemo. I knew that I had to finish chemo to survive, but I also knew that I owed it to Mama and my sisters and my grandmother and all of my family and friends who stuck by me. I felt empowered when I realized I was making a conscious choice to continue chemotherapy.

The other thing that kept me going was Odie. He had been through all of it—the fear, the endless chemo, the emotional distress from being cut out of a normal life. And yet, what had he gotten in return for it? A cure? Health? A few more years? No, Odie had nothing to show for his agony, and somehow, by the grace of God, he remained brave and strong and positive and determined. He remained full of love, and he continued to show his love until the end. Even on his deathbed, Odie never gave up. And there I was, wanting to give up when I was the one with a cure. I knew that I had the passion and desire and intellect needed to help change chemo for kids like Odie and me and many others that I loved so much, and Odie's battle with cancer reaffirmed this for me. I promised myself that I would fight cancer when he couldn't anymore.

EHH

A faithful person could have chosen to end the treatments and so to acquiesce in death. For there are limits to what persons can endure, limits which many people, faithful or not, would simply lack the power of will to suffer through, and there are situations in which the best for a person can be death. If, for example, one's prospects for recovery are nil, or if survival would leave one with no way to practice humanity. In such cases the sufferer may faithfully end the fight to keep life going. Doing so can, in fact, make being overtaken by death into an action of faithful life. And those who love the sufferer may recognize and also consent to her death as her real good, depending on the actual conditions of the sufferer's life. This is not to say that others should take the sufferer's life. And it most certainly does not mean that consenting to the beloved sufferer's death, even desiring it (and at the same time not desiring it), would be without great pain and grief. Most readers will know instances of these very things.

But Maggie chose life, and her choice was a manifestation of the kingdom of God at work. She vividly describes a great swath of emotions. Among them is a strange sense of responsibility for her cancer, a sense of guilt about it. "Everyone was counting on me and I let them down," she says. And "It's all my fault, because it's my body and I'm the one who got cancer. What did I do wrong?" An oncologist friend tells me that such guilt feelings are not uncommon among cancer patients; psychologists surely have much to say about this. But I think we can see in this sense of guilt and responsibility an emotion with spiritual and not only psychological meaning.

Maggie's feeling of guilt grows from her membership in the hidden kingdom, for that membership carries with it the sense that her life was not simply her own, that loving and being loved by her mother, larger family, friends, and those at St. Jude working hard toward her healing made them part of her and her part of them. Fighting cancer, she was not only pursuing her own desire to live, which was now challenged, but the desire others had for her to live and to flourish. That others did desire her healing meant that they had bound a part of their own joy to Maggie. For her part, Maggie also desired the fulfillment of their desire and their joy; that is the way reciprocal loving works. She knew that her life would bring joy to them and not only to herself. Thus, she desired to live *for their sakes*.

The hidden kingdom of God is made real in particular persons by their reciprocal loving. Members, participants in the kingdom, are made members and are made who they are because of other members. Maggie knew this, felt this. Feeling it especially in relation to her mother and to Odie, she chose life. She chose with the knowledge that her prospects for life were good, that life would answer to the desire of others for her good, and that life would allow her to exercise her mind and heart for the sake of Odie and other sufferers of childhood cancer.

Maggie's sense of obligation was strongest for Odie, but she recognizes it as extending to other children and, indeed, to persons unknown. Thus does the hidden kingdom spread beyond her immediate life. Surviving and becoming an oncologist and cancer researcher will not be in time to save the lives of Odie, Carissa, and her other young friends. But it will serve others who are also part of God's world. The desire to serve them reaches into the future and binds her to their lives and them to hers: the joy of the kingdom of heaven lies in just such reciprocity of desire. And the desire to cultivate and contribute to that reciprocity of life is part of faithful life in the hidden kingdom.

Knowingly or not, Maggie's choice of life in spite of suffering is an exercise of faith in which it is not Maggie alone who acts. It is Maggie plus all of those whose desire for her good has given them a part in her life. The choice is not only hers; it is also theirs. And the action is God acting in all their actions. God's eternal action of creative loving is hidden in the particular lives of persons as they bind themselves to each other in desiring the good of the others. It is hidden, but it is present.

The experience that led Maggie almost to discontinue treatment raised all the old questions. Why, God? What did I do to deserve this? Why do some get cancer while others do not? Why is my cancer susceptible to effective treatment while Odie's is not? How does cancer fit into the grand scheme of things?

Maggie did not choose to continue treatment because faith answered these questions. Faith does not eliminate suffering or answer the questions suffering raises. It does not take suffering away, and it does not promise to cure cancer. Faith, in the lived sense in which we have been using the term, does, however, make one a participant in the kingdom where God's eternal action of perfect love is enacted through the reciprocal loving of the participants. Thus—and paradoxically—it brings the joy of the-good-no-matter-what even in the midst of great suffering and grief. Maggie knew this; she experienced it, as her journal shows.

Odie had been very much on Maggie's mind since just before Christmas. Around that time, the time when Maggie experienced most strongly that loving and being loved are the good for which God creates us, Odie and his family received the news that his treatment was not working. He would spend Christmas at home because there was no point in continuing the

treatment. Maggie's awareness of Odie's plight figured large into her decision to continue with her own treatment. The continuation of their friendship through her last months at St. Jude was a big part of her experience.

Odie was dying. What could she do? She could be with Odie and show
him that she cared about him. Being with Odie when she could be and giving him her prayers when she could not be, would be a continuation of the
sacramental experience he had brought into her life in the summer when
she first came to St. Jude. Being with him would be giving both of them
more of the experience of the-good-no-matter-what. It would be giving
both of them more of the experience of God's eternal action of creative love
hidden in the ordinary actions of reciprocal caring between two persons.
It would be making actual in Odie's now short life the value death could
not take away. It would be helping him die in the spirit of gratitude, which
Maggie had come know is the real defeat of death.

We have said that part of faith is the willingness to be changed in order to receive the good God intends for us. Thinking of Odie, Maggie here
declares her willingness, her desire, to be changed into a better person for
him. This common sense of an obligation to be better for the sake of another is a manifestation of the hidden kingdom. It is the sense that another
will somehow receive value from the way we live. It acknowledges that the
other by whom one is inspired desires that we be good at being what and
who we are created to be. Being so will fulfill the other's desire and give
them joy.

MCC, FRIDAY, JANUARY 14, 2011

We got bad news about Odie in late December, right around Christmas. As
snow was falling, Odie learned that he would be home for Christmas; the
doctors were ending his treatment because it wasn't working. When he got
the news, I was in the hospital with shingles, which I had contracted due to
a weak immune system from all of the chemo I'd endured. Patients were not
allowed in my hospital room because I was in isolation. Other cancer patients didn't need to catch shingles. Somehow, some way, my doctors made
an exception for Odie. They knew how much I cared about him, and they
allowed him into my isolation room.

He came in wearing a gown, latex gloves, and a contagious smile. His
dreary prognosis hadn't changed anything about who he was. I filmed Odie
that day on my little digital camcorder. I still have the videos. The most

precious one to me is of Odie saying the words, "I'm really going to miss you, Maggie." I think we both knew he didn't just say that because he was leaving the hospital.

That day in my hospital room was one of my favorite memories of our time together. We laughed and talked and hugged until it was time for him to go home. It was the first time I told Odie that I loved him, and he said it right back without hesitation. Our bond was something understood; he was my little brother now.

Before he left that day, I gave him a ring. It was a special ring, given to me by a former St. Jude patient who'd battled cancer at my age years before. Her name was Emily, and she had gone on to marry and have a child and live a healthy, normal life. Emily had given me the ring at a really difficult time near the beginning of my treatment. She said that whoever gave it to her told her that when they looked at her, they saw strength, which is the word that was engraved in the ring. Emily said that when she looked at me, she also saw strength. When I gave the ring to Odie, I took it out and told him its history. Then I told him that I wanted him to have it because it fit him best. He was stronger than I, stronger than anyone I knew, and I wanted him to stay strong when he went home. Odie wanted to share the ring, though, so we decided to take turns wearing it, and we passed it back and forth every time he came back to St. Jude for a check-up.

As I sit here now, all I can think about is Odie. I don't understand why the universe allows people as kind and gentle and loving as him to get sick, and I really don't understand why it allows those same people to stay sick.

I hope I get to see Odie again in February and that when I see him, he is able to run down the hall to meet me and jump into my arms. On a less selfish note, I hope Odie finds joy at home. I hope he is a stranger to pain and remains close to his family. I hope he is safe and happy and carefree. I hope he is strong and hopeful. That was my Christmas wish, and that is my wish now.

But beyond hoping and wishing, I know, without a doubt, that my friendship with Odie will last . . . forever. And even though I'm not always sure about God or life or how to cope with cancer, I am sure about this. Odie was—and is—my angel. He touched me when I needed it the most and will remain in my heart for eternity. I hope my Christmas wish for Odie has come true, that this Christmas was not only about a baby in a manger but about a little boy getting to go home and be happy. I will try to follow in his example and live every moment to its fullest, with family close by. And maybe I'll get my Christmas wish.

This journal, and every other journal I've published, is dedicated to Odie Harris, my friend and angel. I love you, Odie.

MCC, SUNDAY, JANUARY 16, 2011

It seems I didn't get my biggest Christmas wish . . . yet. Odie isn't doing too well these days from what I hear. I see him all the time, in my thoughts and in my memories. He is what drives me forward into the darkness that chemo is. He is what tugs at my heart and gives me a reason to live. I spend most moments praying for him, the best that I know how these days. He is behind every gust of wind, every rain drop, and every tear that I cry. Sometime I wonder if I'm kidding myself, holding on to this thing that we call hope. But it's really all I have left now. I keep his bracelet on my left wrist and tug at it every time I think of him . . . which is an awful lot.

MCC, TUESDAY, JANUARY 25, 2011

Odie came back to St. Jude after being sent home, and we knew it was probably a bad sign, but we weren't really sure what was going on. I was selfishly happy to see Odie come to St. Jude for a visit. I wanted to know how much time he had left—how much time we had left.

I promised myself that I would be strong for Odie. He was my angel, my everything, my heart, and my life. I sit here and wonder why the prayers didn't work the way we wanted them to. Why didn't the chemo work on him? Why is Odie being taken from me and from his family who loves him so much?

It's weird how fast this experience is coming to an end, how quickly it's going to be over. My biggest fear now, I think, is not failing to recover, but failing to change from all of this. It is not idealism I wish to abandon, nor innocence. It is not sensitivity for the delicacies of this world. I hope that this experience has changed me for the better, however much of a cliche that ideal may be. I *want* to be a different person, a better person, for him. I will be stronger every day because of him.

I don't know how or why, but we connected deeply immediately. Why would God take him from me after something like that? I feel so angry at whatever or whoever controls the world. When I think of Odie the world stops for a little while. I picture the times it was just the two of us, talking and laughing. I hold my hands to my heart and try to stop the aching I feel already.

MCC, MONDAY, FEBRUARY 28, 2011

Odie and his mom returned to the hospital to try an experimental treatment for his cancer. His school had just held an assembly for him and the Marines in his town made him an honorary Marine because he wanted to be one when he grew up. We knew that he probably wouldn't grow up. I always wondered how he handled that. He lived inside every moment, not outside. He lived in the moment.

I was in the hospital with one of many leg infections, and Odie showed up in my room wearing a camouflage Marine outfit, complete with lace-up Marine boots and a camouflage hat. He had grown a lot just since I'd seen him. He looked stronger and healthier than ever, and for a little while I think we all thought that he was beating his cancer.

I've never seen anyone so full of pride. Odie stood before us in his outfit, beaming with honor for his country. It was in that moment that I began to have much more appreciation for the United States military. Odie was beginning to look like a young man. He was no longer the little boy that I'd met months earlier. He even had little hairs sprouting all over his head.

I wasn't allowed to leave the hospital, so Odie, my little sister, and I walked down the hall and played games with some teenage volunteers. We ordered pizza, and I was so happy to see Odie eating it. He really did seem completely healthy. We laughed so much that night as we played game after game with the volunteers. It was the happiest I would ever see Odie.

Not long after that visit, we were shocked to find out that Odie had received more bad news. The experimental treatment hadn't helped, and his cancer was growing even more quickly than before. I will never understand why Odie looked so healthy when he really wasn't. Maybe it was his unbeatable spirit that shone through that day. I spoke to him on the phone, struggling for the right thing to say, for anything at all to say that wouldn't seem completely wrong. I knew that I could no longer understand what he was going through. Odie was the one to break the silence.

"I don't pray a lot, Maggie, but when I do, it's for you," he said selflessly, as if I was the one who needed prayers.

MCC, MARCH 16, 2011

I got to visit my Odie in the hospital yesterday. He had come for a check-up but ended up inpatient with a terrible fever and horrible pains in his stomach. Because Odie's cancer was in his liver, his liver had begun to bleed out into his stomach. The doctors didn't think that he would make it more than a few days longer. I knew that I had to see him. It was time for us to say goodbye. Since Odie was in isolation, he wasn't supposed to have visitors. He had some strange virus on top of everything else, and I wasn't allowed in his room. My doctor and nurse practitioner gave me the best gift they could have given me, though. They allowed me to sneak into his room and see him after I promised to wear a gown, gloves, and a mask.

We had the best meeting we've ever had. We talked about how we imagine heaven, and he even cracked a few jokes.

I couldn't believe that Odie looked so sick when I saw him. He was lying in the bed, his eyes closed, holding onto a morphine pump and squeezing it every few seconds. He was pale, and he had dark circles around his eyes. He was thin, too thin, and he no longer looked like the young Marine I had seen just a month or so earlier. He was a little boy again. I walked into the room alone and sat down in the chair beside his bed. I was scared to speak, worried that I would wake him, and I didn't want to disturb him if he had some ounce of peace left.

"Odie," I said, "I don't want to bother you, so if you don't want to talk, then don't worry about it. I just want to be close to you for a little while."

He slowly opened his eyes and forced a painful smile onto his face. "That's okay, Maggie. I can talk for a little while."

"How are you feeling?" What I stupid question I had just asked.

"Not so good," he said, "Pretty bad, actually."

"I'm so sorry you have to do this," I said to him as the tears began to well up in my eyes. "I'm so sorry."

"It's okay, Maggie. It's not your fault," he answered, wise beyond his years.

I looked at him for a little while, feeling comfortable in the silence. I put my gloved hand on his bedside. "Are you scared, Odie?"

"No, not really, not for me. I'm scared to leave my mom behind, and to leave you. But I know that I'll be okay. I know that I'm going to go to heaven." I wondered how he could be so brave while he was dying. I was the one who was afraid. I was the one who doubted everything.

"What do you think heaven is like?" I asked him, managing to smile for a moment.

"I think I'll get to play video games all day every day and eat but never get full."

"That would be great," I said, realizing that he was the one comforting me.

"Yeah, but heaven will probably be different for you, because you don't play video games."

"Maybe so," I said, "but I bet we'll see each other there."

He sighed, squeezing the pain medicine pump once again, a look of agony on his face. I could tell he was miserable.

"I'm going to miss you so much, Odie," I said, tears running down my face.

"Please don't cry, Maggie," he said. I held myself together for him, knowing that I had to stop crying because he needed me to. I wiped away the tears and looked at him again.

"I love you so much, Odie."

"I love you too, Maggie." He said it as if it was the most obvious thing in the world, and for a tiny moment, he looked happy again.

"You know, having cancer was worth it because I got to meet you," I said, meaning every word.

"Having cancer was worth it because I got to meet you, too," he said, and I realized that he knew he was dying. I couldn't hold back the tears any longer, so I let them flow.

"I love you to the moon and back," I whispered.

"I love you to the moon and back infinity times," he smiled.

I smiled and looked down at my lap, not knowing what to say next. I looked up and saw that he was wearing our ring on a chain around his neck. *Strength*. It described him completely.

"You know? My only regret is dying a virgin," he said with a huge smile on his face. I started laughing, and I know that's what he wanted. Even in the face of death, he was making me laugh.

"I'm going to be a doctor for kids like us one day. I'm going to try to change things," I said.

"I know, Maggie," he looked at me for a moment.

"I'm going to let you rest now," I said, noticing the way he had begun to wince again. I stood up, leaned over him, and kissed him on the forehead. Then I walked out of the dark room.

EHH

After Maggie's most poignant visit with Odie, she had but one chemo treatment to go. It was delayed because of low platelet counts, which was frustrating, although something she and her mother had grown accustomed to. As they waited for her counts to come up, Maggie confronted the anger she had been feeling. She had discussed it with her chaplain Lisa Anderson and with Andy Andrews and had expressed it from time to time in her journal; indeed, it was always just under the surface. Now the awful experiences that had overtaken her in January and the sad prognosis for Odie made Maggie feel the anger more strongly than ever. It found its way into the content and underlying negative tone of her journal, making some of her readers ask what had happened. She felt reproved and took up the subject with her psychologist. Was she wrong to be angry? She received wise counsel. Anger, the psychologist insisted, is a constructive emotion. She should not feel guilty about it.

MCC, FRIDAY, MARCH 25, 2011

I have been very angry for a long time now, and I think it's because I didn't have any feelings at all when I first found out I had cancer. I feel absolutely horrible right now, and it's all because I have been so angry and negative. I had no right to dump all of that on you, and I am so sorry. I am trying my best to move past it now and move forward, and I know I will. I hope I have not offended anyone with my negativity, but it's over now. I hope I will learn from my mistake.

I have made so many friends in the past ten months! We have had a blast getting to know everyone, and I have loved getting closer to my friends and family. I am looking forward to being back at St. Jude in May for my research and going back to Rhodes in the fall. I am going to have a wonderful and happy life! I will use this experience in the future to help others in my position because I know how they will feel.

I love how Dr. Lemos put it when she said, "Don't ever apologize for being angry about this. You have every right to be angry and to feel whatever you want to feel. Don't get sucked into the pressure to smile all the time as if what you have undergone has not been a tremendous struggle and burden. Yes, you have and will overcome it, but who is to say that your anger is not part of that? Anger has driven social and personal change in so many cases throughout the world. Anger is a constructive emotion. Passion is so much of what makes life worth living—and part of passion is having negative responses to things that are difficult or wrong. You have every right to feel whatever you feel."

It is hard to have a change of heart overnight or when people tell you that you should be positive. Yes, but I now believe that pretending to be positive leads to positivity. Haven't you heard that using the muscles that are used to smile releases endorphins in your brain? Endorphins make people happy. So try it!

I have always been passionate about things in life. Someone once said in a movie, *Country Strong*, to find as many things in life to love as possible because it's all that matters in life. I agree, and there are many things and people that I am in love with in this world. They include sequins, elephants, my grandmother Anne, my friend Beth, my doctors, St. Jude, Rhodes College, squirrels, candy, writing, yoga, piano, chemistry, mock trial, acting, karaoke, food . . . and much more. These are the things that keep me alive.

EHH

Maggie had, I believe, all along made anger a part of her attitude of faith. Now, after it had become more of a drag on the recovery process than a motivation for it, she became intentional about using it constructively.

Rightly directed, anger is an outworking of love. If one loves the right things, one will feel anger at the right things. In the life of the hidden kingdom, one is seeking to love God and one's neighbors. Loving God means desiring what God desires. Desiring what God desires should make one, therefore, angry about anything that militates against what God desires, whether it be in oneself or in another or in the world at large. Loving one's neighbor should make one angry about whatever interferes with or diminishes the good God desires for them. Faithful persons ought to feel anger about disease, catastrophe, injustice, and moral corruption of all kinds. Not to feel anger would mean apathy, indifference, spiritual and moral laziness. To feel anger, on the other hand, is to be motivated and energized to act.

We can see anger working constructively in Maggie as she fights through the pain and the disappointment that almost made her give up chemotherapy. We can see anger working constructively as Maggie determines not to give way to despair but to focus on the good things she loves. And we can see anger working constructively as she hurts for Odie and dedicates herself to a life of medical practice and research to combat childhood cancer.

What about anger with God? Can anger with God be an expression of faith? Surely it can be, for it recognizes God and prevents indifference; it energizes one to engage with God. Anger at God often flows from the sense that God is the Grand Cosmic Engineer with infinite coercive power tucked up the divine sleeve and ready to bring about whatever changes in the world God may deem desirable. On that understanding of God, one would reasonably expect God to magically change the world to eliminate one's disease. And when God does not do so, one would reasonably be angry at God if he did not. But the more one realizes that God is not that Cosmic Engineer, the less will one expect God simply to eliminate the disease and the less likely one will be to be angry with God for not doing so.

Nevertheless, the faithful who do not operate with the Cosmic Engineer idea may rightly pray for healing and still feel angry with God when it does not come. What then? Can their anger still be an expression of faithful life? The pastoral answer is that there is nothing wrong with anger at God. God can take it and will suffer through our emotional distress with us and bring us to a point of balance. Witness C. S. Lewis's *A Grief Observed*. Anger expresses a love of God if it energizes engagement with God and life in the hidden kingdom. In Maggie's experience the anger is problematical when it operates to justify negativity, making her lose energy for going on. When she is assured that it is appropriate and that it can be a constructive emotion in bringing about change, she sets about to use it in that constructive way. It becomes energy for reentering the life of reciprocal loving.

At last Maggie's counts came up enough for her final chemotherapy treatment. It was completed on March 30. However, there was one last frightening set back. It was another leg infection and apparently far more serious than the previous ones.

MCC, FRIDAY, APRIL 8, 2011

I had completed the last treatment. I was ready to walk out of St. Jude and back into my normal life! Then, back in my bed at Target House and resting up from the past few days of chemo, I felt a pain in my leg. It was so strong that I couldn't move. My leg was hurting the way it used to hurt right before we found out I had cancer—only much worse. It made me think one thing: the cancer was back. I panicked. We went straight to the hospital. I got an

X-Ray, and it showed nothing, but it didn't show anything the first time, either, so that only scared us more.

After running some additional tests and taking my temperature, the doctors concluded that I had a serious infection in my prosthesis and that it required an immediate operation to wash it out.

Back I went into the hospital. I lay there for a couple of days while the doctors debated what to do with me. I was sent into my second leg surgery, and my scar was opened about halfway, five inches. The fluid in my leg was drained, and the surgeons washed out my prosthesis to try to get rid of any infection. They also removed the source of infection, my port. We were able to remove it because I was finished with chemotherapy.

When I came out of surgery, I wanted to know the same thing I wanted to know after the first surgery: Did we still have my leg? In a major leg surgery, there is always the possibility of losing the leg. Thanks to my wonderful doctors, I woke up with both legs for the second time. When I thought things would finally get better, they got worse. With no port, all of my medicines and fluids had to be given intravenously. To make matters worse, I have terrible veins. They roll, burst, and hide. A few times a day, a team of nurses would come into the room and attempt to stick me in one of my veins. There were only a couple times that it worked. They even had to use my hands and threatened to use my feet. After a long weekend, with little sleep and lots of Ativan, I was given a PICC line in my right bicep area, which works like a port but is shorter term. The sticking stopped.

The fever keeps coming, however, and no one can be sure exactly why. We hope it's because my body is fighting off the infection in my leg, but we can't even prove that my leg is infected. I am now on two antibiotics, one IV, and one oral. The oral one turns all my bodily fluids, including my tears, red. It also makes me sick. As a result, my weight has gone below the ideal.

The only way I know how to get through this at all is to take it one day at a time. When I get up in the morning, one day seems like too much. One moment, though, is something I can bear. My mother is by my side 100 percent of the time. She gives me the will and the strength to keep fighting, even though the end isn't in sight anymore.

My plan is to keep on going, no matter what. I am taking my medicine, keeping my leg dry, and working harder than ever in physical therapy. That is all I can do.

Someone once told me that God doesn't give us anything we can't handle. I hope that this is true. I hope that I can handle this. But I am not going to attempt to handle it alone. I need all the hope, love, and prayers I can get.

I feel like I have strength today, like everything will be okay eventually, soon even. I feel like there is a God and God does answer prayers, even if it takes him or her an awfully long time. My heart aches for Odie because I miss him dearly, but he is coming to St. Jude next week for the formal. Flynn is also going, and we have picked her out a beautiful dress that the Tri Deltas donated to St. Jude. I hope she likes it when she gets back from the horse show.

MCC, JUNE, 2011

I spent a couple of weeks in the hospital after my second surgery, and I spent most of that time crying about what had happened. I don't know how my mother put up with that part of the experience, to be honest. It had to be hard to watch. By the time I had come to the end of the chemotherapy I was walking well and without any obvious limp. Now, after my leg was washed out, I couldn't even put my foot on the ground. I had to start physical therapy all over again. I felt defeated, and after seven months of hard work, I had absolutely nothing to show for it. Before the infection, I was bending my leg over one hundred degrees. After the surgery, I was back down to fifty degrees. I felt like I had no fight left in me. I was embarrassed to be on crutches again, and I wondered if I'd ever get my walk back to where it was. I had to start from square one after the surgery. I cannot walk anymore, and I am using crutches and a wheelchair again. I have never been so frustrated in my life.

I worked hard with my physical therapist Kristin. I also worked harder than I ever had on my own. I did my leg exercises every day, and sometimes twice a day if I had the time and energy. There was pain. There were moments when I felt completely discouraged. There were times when I still grieved over what I had lost. God only knows how much of my complaining and grieving Kristin had to put up with. But each time I wanted to give up, I kept working at it and was able to get my walking back to where it was before the infection and surgery.

EHH

Even worse than having to go through the pain and effort of physical therapy all over again was the depression into which this last setback and delay had thrown Maggie. Andy Andrews became especially important to her during this time. She had counseled with him since the previous summer, but now she needed his spiritual wisdom more than ever.

MCC, WEDNESDAY, APRIL 13, 2011

I was intensely afraid when this infection came on me. The cultures of the fluid in my leg never came back positive for infection, but the infection count in my blood work continued to rise, and the pain in my leg was excruciating. The doctors didn't know what was going on. I would wake up in the middle of the night and begin to cry, scared that I wasn't going to make it, that after a long year of chemo, something terrible had gone wrong.

I have never been so afraid for my life, not even when I was diagnosed with cancer. You see, this time I could feel *death*. Somehow I knew that it wasn't far away. The MRI showed no cancer, but my body was becoming septic. The doctors arrived each morning at the crack of dawn to inform us that the cultures of my infected leg taken during surgery the week before continued to show no signs of bacterial growth. It appeared that my leg and more and more of my body were grossly infected, but there was no proof in the laboratory that this was the case. The infection was a mystery.

One night, as my fever climbed above 102 and my body shook with chills, I dreamed several dreams. In the first dream, my bad leg was stuck under an iceberg, and I couldn't get out. In the second dream, my leg was stuck in some rocks somewhere on a beach, sand everywhere. In the third dream, I was actually dying in a hospital bed somewhere and there was only one emotion: fear. Fear enveloped me completely, escalating to terror. It was like falling off a cliff, plunging into darkness, leaving everything that is comforting.

They say that we never die in our dreams; they say we must wake up before we actually dream that we have died. Well, they are wrong. In this dream, on this particular night, I died all the way. It is hard to describe the sensation that followed. Words are quite inadequate when it comes to describing something as ephemeral as a dream. The feelings were real. The terror was real. The pain and anguish and guilt and sadness and desperation were palpable and overwhelming. Yet the moment the act of dying had it-self passed, everything changed.

It was like a dark room. I couldn't see a thing. But it was much more than a dark room. In that space, or in that exception to space, I felt peaceful. The pain, gone. The anguish, gone. The sadness, lifted from me like a warm coat on a hot day. I was free again. And above all, I was completely and indescribably "*unalone*." Not a single tangible *body* or *thing* was present, but *everyone was there*. Every single soul I had ever loved or associated with or even crossed paths with was there, not only surrounding me but combining with me. It was as if my very *self* had become only the parts of it that are capable of love, as if I was one with all the souls around, and we were part of something spectacular. It was eternal.

I woke up at some point. Eventually my fears subsided as my body responded to the antibiotics pumping through my bloodstream. I began to heal. I am not claiming to have died and gone to heaven or even to have dreamed of heaven. I do believe, however, that whatever I experienced was as real and true as things get.

EHH

Maggie's dream was a "vision," "seeing" beyond the ordinary into its spiri-tual meaning. She was seeing beyond the experiences she had been having of loving and of being loved and of knowing that God is in the reciprocal exchanging. The experience of reciprocal loving had so far been that God is hidden in the ordinary lives of persons insofar as they manage to love and to receive love, but that the kingdom remains partial and occluded because of the failures of love. Now, feeling death to be near, she sees what the perfection of the kingdom might be like. Her experience of the-good-no-matter-what seems to be confirmed. Persons would be "completely and indescribably 'unalone'"; they would be "combined" with one another and every soul would be "only the parts of it that are capable of love . . ." This would no longer be reciprocity; it would be union. Yet it seems that, since everyone would be there, personal identity would not be dissolved. What-ever we make of Maggie's dream vision, it seems to put a bold exclamation point on the conviction that the highest good, the good that beats cancer and disease, the good God desires us to have, is participation in the king-dom of mutual love.

Maggie's journal did not end with the description of the dreams. It continued. The relationship she had built with Andy Andrews now became especially important.

MCC, FRIDAY, APRIL 15, 2011

Andy Andrews visited me several times during the struggle with this anxiety. I cried to him and told him about my fears: infection and cancer and death. I described my dreams to him and explained that the doctors didn't exactly know what was wrong with my leg. Andy was his usual self on these visits: calm and gentle and loving. He listened to everything without telling me that I was wrong or being silly or crazy. He seemed to understand.

We started talking about death, and he told me that he'd sensed death before. He said that when people were dying, he usually got a certain feeling around them and that he didn't feel that way around me. Then we started talking about God and how the conventional ways of viewing God didn't always work for me. When we realized that we were both vegetarians, we got on the topic of animals. I told Andy that I often saw God in animals, that I saw him in dogs sometimes. I had never shared such an "off-the-shelf" idea about my spirituality with anyone before, and I half expected Andy to laugh or tell me that I was wrong. But I looked up and saw a tear running down his face. He was touched. The truth is that I saw a whole lot of God in Andy.

Another time I asked him how he knew that God was real and that even if God was real, how could I know God cared about me. He told about his childhood, about his sometimes hot-tempered father, and a mother who loved him unconditionally and protected him. He talked about how his mother would always pick up the pieces of him that his father had shattered and put him back to together. After his father's rages, his mother would hold him and praise him and heal him, again and again. He said the love his mother showed him was God.

I've thought about that story many times since it was told to me, and it seems to me that the story is not only a true event but also a metaphor for God's love. The world presents us with pain, whether it comes from abuse, our own mistakes, or even cancer. But time and time again, God is there to pick us up and put us back together. Whether God is in a loving, self-sacrificing mother, in a priest who listens, or even in a playful dog, God is there to heal us. Sometimes we just have to look for him or her.

EHH

"God is there to heal us. Sometimes we just have to look for him or her." Yes, God is ever present but hidden. Being aware of the presence is the hard part. God does not act by forcing a grand blueprint on creation, by determining every event and every reaction to every event, by assigning terrible pain and suffering to some and easy lives to others. But God creates us to live our lives as who we ourselves are and can be. When we respond to the hard things faithfully, our responses are sacramental. They participate in the eternal love of God; they make God present in the world. And God works good in those who respond faithfully to the events of life. God, then, is not a magician who simply removes the suffering that comes to us, but God makes use of the suffering when we are able to cooperate with God in God's desire for our ultimate good.

God's healing for Odie and God's healing for Maggie are different yet the same. Odie's faithful response is accepting the unwanted in a spirit of gratitude and trust. Doing so, he experiences the-good-no-matter-what and, in the way possible for him, lives his life in God, and manifests the hidden kingdom. Maggie's faithful response is receiving the cure and the promise of a life serving the needs of children with cancer. She, too, knows the-good-no-matter-what, lives life in God, and manifests the hidden kingdom.

The life of faith does not take away disease, disaster, pain, anguish, uncertainty, and doubt. But it does give the experience of the-good-no-matter-what and of joy even in the middle of life's pains and anguish. Faith grows from the hidden seed of the kind of love that is desire for the good of the other. It is supported and strengthened when persons in community live that kind of love together. This love that is the seed from which the kingdom grows can be deformed and destroyed, even turned to hate. But it can also be expanded and extended. "Love your neighbor as yourself." Indeed, "love your enemies."

The growth of life in the hidden kingdom is the work of a lifetime. It can be encouraged, cultivated, supported, and given shape by the sacred texts, ideas, and practices of religious institutions. On the other hand, and we see it far too much among "religious" people, persons can use those texts, ideas, and practices in ways that choke the life of God and destroy possible expressions of the hidden kingdom. Maggie's experience, and that of her family and friends and of the care givers at St. Jude, lay bare for us the presence of the eternal and perfect love of God, which is hidden in their lives and relationships during Maggie's year at St. Jude. That love is the eternal action by which God creates and sustains all that there is. We have but to pay attention in order to see it.

The treatment of Maggie's last leg infection, her hard work to recover the ability to walk again, and her struggle through depression and frustration bring her to the brink of her return to "regular" life.

MCC, WEDNESDAY, APRIL 20, 2011

I had scans all day Monday. I can't remember ever feeling so nervous about a test result since after my surgery. Even though my tumor was 100 percent dead upon removal, I couldn't help but wonder if it was too good to be true. I couldn't help but wonder if the cancer had found a way to creep back, the way it does to so many amazing people. My scans were all completely clear. I thought that hearing news like that would make me want to jump up and down, celebrate, cry even. But I felt the same way I felt right after my diagnosis: empty, shocked, numb. It isn't like me at all not to feel in response to situations. I know that I have so much to be thankful for, and I just received the best news in the universe. I am so grateful. I think that my feelings will follow soon. Right now, I guess it seems too good to be true, especially when so many friends of mine here don't seem to get the good news I get.

It really isn't fair. I don't know why we spend so much time complaining about how the world isn't fair. I don't know who ever told us it would be. Perhaps it was the board games we played as children or the lines we waited in as we took turns being the leader. We were just taught to think everything goes by rules of fairness. But nothing about real life seems to work that way. I guess that's where grace comes in.

Yesterday I got an MRI because an X-Ray showed a potential fracture in my femur where the prosthesis enters it. My doctors assured me that there was a very tiny chance that it was fractured, so I haven't been that worried about it. It would be a nice problem to have compared to the infection or to cancer. While I was lying on the MRI table, my arms straight down by my sides, headphones on, music playing in the background, I started to cry.

It was the first bit of emotional relief I've felt since the scans came back so perfectly. I silently thanked God, the universe, and my body for healing. I can't believe that about a year ago I was diagnosed with childhood cancer. I don't know that it will ever seem completely real to me. All I know is that I am cured now, and that makes me the luckiest girl in the world. I'm going to get a second chance. That's more than a lot of people can say. As I write this, I am overwhelmed with emotion and disbelief simultaneously. I did it. We did it. And even though I have an infected leg, I am so proud of my determination and my body. I am even thankful for chemotherapy.

A few days ago, just after my twentieth birthday and even though I was anxious, Mama, Flynn, and I went to a very strange movie (*Hannah*). Then we went into a bookstore. As we walked through the doors, I limped along with my bag of IV fluids hanging off of me. A man locked eyes with me. I noticed that, he too, was limping. But he was also twitching violently, as if he had Tourette's Syndrome. Instead of averting his eyes, as so many people do when they see my bald head, my limp, and my IV fluids, the man smiled at me. Then he stopped walking, looked straight at me, and said, "Hello. How are you?" I smiled at him and told him that I was well. I asked him how he was doing, and he said that he was also well. Then our paths went their separate directions, most likely never to cross again, the way paths do in this world.

For whatever reasons, I couldn't get my interaction with this strange man out of my head. Perhaps it was because we both have a limp, or because we are both different from most of the population. Perhaps it is because we are both all too used to being stared at. Or maybe, our kindness towards one another allowed us to glimpse a little bit of grace, a tiny ounce of God, a rare thing to grasp in our busy world.

I am not the type of person who usually feels God's presence while I am reading Scripture or singing hymns. I envy and admire the people who have these gifts. But I do see supernatural beauty in my mother's embrace, my little sister's laugh, and the conversations I have with my priest. I do feel God in friendship, healing, and karaoke. I sense the Holy Spirit in my friends, doctors, and fellow cancer-warriors. And that, I think, is grace.

MCC, MONDAY, APRIL 25, 2011

One of my favorite things about my oncologist, Dr. Pappo, is the way he speaks. He was born and raised in Mexico, so he has a strong accent, and sometimes his grammar is a little off. I wouldn't have it any other way. A few weeks ago, when I had intense pain in my leg due to the infection, I told Dr. Pappo that I was worried the cancer was back. His response? "Ain't no tumor in there." Today, I showed him a few bruises on my arms and legs from when my platelets were low and told him I was worried I had secondary leukemia. His response was, "Ain't no secondary leukemia in there." When I asked him how his gout was doing, he said, "Ain't no mo gout in there."

We got good news today. My CRP, C-reactive protein, an inflammatory marker that often corresponds with infection, is down from 7 to 1.5. Normal is 1. Next week, when it goes down to 1 and I am done with all of my follow up appointments at St. Jude, I will get off of my IV antibiotics and go home . . . for real. I will move out of the Target House and really go home. I can't believe it.

But with good news comes a thick feeling of nostalgia. We've lived here for almost an entire year now. Our best friends are people here: the doctors, nurses, patients, and families that fill the halls of Target House and St. Jude. When we leave next week, we will be moving away from them.

I've had to deal with several intense goodbyes in my lifetime. I went to Governor's School for a month, Duke Divinity School for a few weeks, and then the pinnacle of it all: Pageland, my experience as a U.S. House Page in D.C. for an entire semester. The thing about those goodbyes is that we didn't know if we were saying goodbye forever, which is the hardest kind of goodbye. When I said goodbye to Odie last time he was here, it felt a little like that. There is no consolation prize except the possibility of an afterlife, a miracle, or sometimes just a memory. Luckily, when we leave St. Jude it won't be for good. I'll be back for checkups every few months at least. But it isn't a foolproof system. Some of the patients here will get better or worse and may not be here when we come back.

I don't know what the solution is to hard goodbyes. Temporary goodbyes are easier and usually done with hugs and kisses and waves. But the kind of goodbye that is more difficult, the more permanent kind . . . I don't know. I usually find myself in tears, begging my body to wake up from a bad dream that isn't a dream at all. When I came home from being a page in D.C., where I met the best friends in the world, I felt like a part of me was dying, fading away like a wilting flower that needs water. And I thought to myself, "I wish I had never met these people. Then it would be easier." Milliseconds later, I realized I was lying to myself. I realized that meeting people who change your life—who change you—is beautiful, even if you have to say goodbye, as you inevitably will one day.

My counselor at the House Page School helped me come to this realization. He said that people come into our lives wherever we go, and every time we make contact with people they change us in some way. They fulfill some purpose in our lives and us in theirs. And when their purpose is complete, they move on. We move on. Everyone moves on. We move on to different places and meet different people and get changed and change others all over again. The goodbyes are never easy, but they are worth the tears.

I will always remember Dr. Pappo's grammar, the way he reassured me, and his sense of humor and belief that laughter is the best medicine. I will always cherish Patti's maternal nurturing, our talks about body image, and our love of *Mean Girls*. I will always smile at myself when I think of Julie's hugs, the bright colors of her scrubs, the gossip we shared, and the way she laughed.

And even if it hurts to leave them and many others, meeting them was so worth it.

9

Something I Can't See

MCC, SUNDAY, MAY 1, 2011

When you find out you have cancer, you abandon all the control you'd ever had and face the "realest" thing you've ever faced. Your world stopped moving. Then, when you finally realize that you are in remission, whether it's official (five years of clear scans) or not, your heart skips a beat. You wonder, "Why me?" and ask God why you are so lucky when some of your friends are not. You realize that you are in the percentage that you worried you might not be in, that you are a survivor, that you are cured. You repeat the word 'cured' over and over again in your head, and even though you know you are happy, you can't feel anything because you don't really believe that this has happened to you. You still can't believe you ever got cancer in the first place. Surely not you. You're normal, healthy, lucky. You've always taken care of yourself. You are a good person. You don't deserve this at all. It takes whomever it pleases. You begin to have random bursts of emotion, exploding into tears randomly as feelings creep up your throat and pour out of your eyes. You can't say the words, "I finished chemo" or "I'm cured," without breaking down and feeling your knees get shaky. In a span of a few seconds, you see the past year in its entirety flash past you, and it's as though you're in an impossibly long dream again. You can't stop the tears from rolling down your cheeks; your teeth are chattering and everyone thinks you are sad. You begin to wonder. Are you experiencing sadness. Why?

Suddenly, you catch your breath. You realize that you made it, that you're getting another chance at life, for whatever reason or no reason at all. You realize that you knew all along that you would be okay in some way, because you've always believed in yourself. You want to hug yourself and worship God and thank all the people who helped you along the way, because there were sure a lot of them. You want to dance on your metal leg, climb a tree, and order a margarita. You want to laugh hysterically, spin around in circles, and drive really, really fast (but carefully). You want to cure cancer and know that you will because if you could beat it then surely you can annihilate it for good. And finally, you want to be still. You want to stare at space in peace and quiet. You close your eyes and take deep breaths, stare at the wall, and ponder the meaning of life. You want to do it right this time, whatever that means. But mostly, you realize that you are not the same person you were when you were diagnosed. Yes, you are much thinner and you have no hair. But you do have a thirteen-inch scar on your right leg, and you are much older, much wiser, and much more capable of true emotion. And as hard as it is to admit, you never would have gotten there without cancer.

Though it would have been hard to agree with such a thing while I was going through cancer, today I can look back at all of it and honestly say that I wouldn't change what happened to me if I could. Without cancer, I never would have met Odie, Dr. Pappo, Patti, Julie, Beth, Lisa, Christina, and so many others I came to love. Without cancer I might not have found my life calling: to be a pediatric oncologist and cancer researcher. I certainly wouldn't have been able to look at my future patients and say, "I understand what you're going through."

Without cancer I wouldn't have gotten to spend another year with my family, growing closer than ever. Without cancer I would have taken my life for granted. Of course, I will always worry a little bit that my cancer may come back, and sometimes I have to remind myself how lucky I am, but I will never forget how much I grew during my battle with cancer.

Cancer didn't settle all my doubts and questions about faith and the world. It didn't solve all my problems or make me want to stop searching and learning. But it did give me a glimpse of something big, important, beautiful, and sacred. Because during my battle, I was touched by a hospital and people so loving that I can only describe their love as "from out of this world."

MCC, JUNE, 2011

The last time I saw Odie alive was at the St. Jude prom last April. He was wearing his formal Marine outfit and looked like a million bucks. My little sister was his date, wearing a long strapless silk gown that had every color of the rainbow on it. She looked grown up and was the most beautiful girl there. We stood outside of Target House and took pictures of the two of them, and I managed to be in some of them, even though I was wearing sweats and a St. Jude t-shirt. I could tell Odie was excited to be going to a prom with a beautiful girl. He pushed me around in my wheelchair as everyone stood around and waited for the limousine. The last time I saw Odie, he was a smiling Marine again.

When my treatment had finally ended, I came home to my Mississippi town to heal. My days are full of reading, naps, and eating the food that Mama made for me. I was still in bed when we got the call. Odie passed away on May 31, 2011, in his bedroom at home, in his mother's arms. I heard the news and closed my eyes, choosing to remain in denial. I woke up later that day, intuitively reaching for my cell phone so that I could text Odie and check on him. That was when it hit me. Not knowing what else to do, I wrote him a letter.

When I went to his funeral a week later, I brought the letter with me. As I stood next to his mother in the church where the visitation was held, I looked ahead at his open casket. "May I put this up there for him?" I asked, showing her the letter. Without a word, she led me to the casket. "You can put it in his hand," she said. As I touched his cold skin, I became aware that the body in the casket was no longer Odie; it was too cold, too vacant. Odie was somewhere else. Still, it felt like the best thing to do. I put the folded up, handwritten note in his hand, kissed my fingers, and pressed them to his forehead.

People tell me a lot that I am "strong," that I am a hero because I survived childhood cancer. But surviving is not what makes someone a hero. I don't know anyone who wouldn't have done what I did that year, anyone who wouldn't have taken their medications and received chemotherapy and surgeries recommended to them by their doctors. It was the only chance I had at surviving. You would do it too, I'm sure. But I did learn a lot about strength that year. I was touched by it, time and time again. There was strength in my mother, as she held me in her arms time and time again and comforted me, by my side all the time. There was strength in my little sister, as she left our home to be homeschooled for a year and help my mother take care of me. Most of all, there was strength in Odie.

In Odie, this strength was something intangible that allowed him to continue experiencing and enjoying life and the people around him, despite his ominous future, which hung over him like a black cloud. Odie's strength allowed him to be selfless, to teach people he came in contact with in this world, even though he knew he was departing from it. Odie's strength was transcendent and godly. It was something from out of this world. When I look for it, I can still see it all around me.

MCC, AUGUST 20, 2011.

There are moments, like this one, that feel like too much. Another dear friend from St. Jude, a fellow patient named Carissa, passed away today. Feeling this way, feeling so tied to death through love, takes me right back to losing Odie just a few months ago, and all I can do is wonder, "Why?" "Why this girl? Why that little boy? Why did they get the types of pediatric cancer that don't respond as well to chemo?" And then, the biggest question of all: "Why am I alive when they aren't?"

Carissa was a St. Jude patient for nearly three years. Can you imagine going through cancer treatment for three years? I can't even imagine going through it for one year, and I've done that. But every time we saw Carissa, she was smiling. She never complained. She never pouted. She never took her anger out on other people. She just lived each day, never failing to offer me comfort when I got another leg infection, when she was the one who needed comfort.

I leave for college again in the morning, and I am full up of emotions. I feel like I may overflow any second. I'm so happy to be getting another chance at life, to be going back with all my friends to a school I love. I'll even get to start my research at St. Jude (finally). But I feel so torn. Being at school means being back in the real world as an adult, on my own, away from my family. It didn't feel like such a big deal the first time I went to college, but it's amazing how much bonding you do when you go through cancer together. Now, I feel like much of who I am lies in them. I feel like being apart from them will be physically painful. I just can't fathom it. I worry that people will be different at college now that I've changed and they've changed. And I know that's only natural, but I feel like I need something to cling to, something constant and unchanging.

Second Corinthians 4:18 says "So we fix our eyes not on what is seen, but on what is unseen. For what is seen is temporary, but what is unseen is eternal." I like this passage because I think it applies to everyone, no matter what their religion is. The only thing I have to cling to is something I can't see or touch or hold in my hands. The only thing that will be constant in my life from here on out—and even after that—is something that words can't describe or name. It is God.

No matter how much thinking or studying I do, there will always be things about God that I am unsure of. But what I am sure of is this: God is real and eternal and invisible and inside of other people. God is what keeps me connected to Odie and Carissa and baby Kya. God is the glue that ties all of my life together. And if I only look for him around me—in nature, in animals, and in people—he will show up, even when I least expect it.

10

Epilogue
Embracing Darkness, Seeing Light

MCC, JUNE, 2014

Four years have passed since my diagnosis with cancer. Sometimes I think back to those few days after my cancer diagnosis before I arrived at St. Jude, the days when I truly thought I would never get to graduate from college, go to medical school, fall in love, plan my wedding, become a doctor, and raise a family of my own. And then I open my eyes, and I realize most of those things are happening right now.

Just two short months after leaving St. Jude, I returned to Rhodes College to resume my education. The transition into the "real world"—a world so different from St. Jude, a world that didn't have at its center children sitting on the edge of life—was incredibly difficult. While the suffering I experienced during treatment was more constant, recovery was sometimes just as trying. Recovery, I realized in time, is a process. Like life and faith, recovery has been a journey for me.

It was difficult to return to normal life after St. Jude. Though I was cancer free, I was leaving a place that had shared much of life with me. It was as if I had spent a year in a place free of pessimism or anger, jealousy or hatred, a place free of judgment, prejudice, or pressure, a place full of strength. And even though I have been out of treatment for over two and a half years, some days I find myself missing it—not the cancer, but the strength that was in the air we breathed there. This is strength that I hold onto, strength that I try not to forget, strength that I would like to adopt when I am a doctor one day.

Upon my return to Rhodes College, I finally began the scientific research I'd been selected to do at St. Jude. I spent two semesters and the following summer in a lab researching stem cell and cord blood oncology, gaining many technical laboratory skills and learning what basic science research was like. I spent two more semesters and another summer in a different laboratory, trying my hand at organic chemistry synthesis based on my love for chemistry. This was a very enriching experience for me, for my clumsiness eventually led to my mentor assigning me a "non-tactile" project. I was allowed to write a review article on anti-malarial therapeutics to be used in a medicinal chemistry textbook. This was my first publication, and I greatly appreciate the principal investigator who guided me throughout this project. My two years in the labs at St. Jude allowed me to stay connected to the hospital. It was unique to be on the employee side of St. Jude rather than the patient one, and on many days, I felt a little guilty and a lot nostalgic as I walked the halls of my beloved hospital, no longer with a hospital bracelet on my wrist.

Being there, however, did allow me to maintain close relationships with my doctors and other caregivers at St. Jude. On many occasions, I was even given the opportunity to shadow Dr. Pappo and other oncologists, gaining more and more confidence in my dream of becoming a physician and maybe even a pediatric oncologist. Upon completing the review article, I contacted a couple of doctors who worked on the Palliative Care team at St. Jude and asked if I might be involved in any of their writing projects; I'd found that my love for writing could be combined with my love for scientific research. Dr. Baker and Dr. Johnson were kind enough to allow me to help author a chapter for the *Pediatric Journal of North America* on end of life care for hospitalized children. I was assigned the sections on spirituality and religion as well as grief and bereavement. This was an incredibly fulfilling project. It allowed me to explore the field of palliative care and use my writing in a meaningful way in the scientific community. It also confirmed my interest in clinical research.

The remaining three years of my time at Rhodes were beautiful, yet far from perfect. The aspect of recovery that was perhaps most difficult for me was finding a way to savor and celebrate life with my renewed perspective while balancing the stresses and anxieties of a "normal" college student. This is still a tension I am learning to live with—allowing myself to have problems that are not cancer without being angry at myself for having these petty and insignificant problems. I think my last few years of college taught me that the key to living well and with renewed perspective is patience—patience with others, patience with God, and most of all, patience with myself. There have been times when my eagerness to savor this fragile and unguaranteed life has led me to desire and expect a perfect life. If there is anything that I know for certain, though, nothing in life is perfect—except love, maybe.

In one of my readings for school during my last semester, I came across some passages about darkness and how it can be a way to find light. I think it's interesting to think of darkness in this way. I don't always buy into the ideas behind Stoic philosophy, that all of our hardships make us stronger, for example; and there are few things I detest more than the saying that "everything happens for a reason." Let's face it, children do not always get cancer *for a reason* or *purpose*. Sometimes our bodies just screw up. Sometimes our genes mutate. But this is not to say that God doesn't act in mysterious ways.

The reading reminded me of the first time I met with my St. Jude chaplain, Lisa Anderson. I sat down, and unable to pretend anymore, I ranted about how angry I was with God, and even more, with the people who kept telling me that "God had a plan for me." When I had finished, I asked her how she could believe in God at a place like St. Jude, and though I am unable to repeat her exact words, what she said in response has never left me. She said that an absence of bad in the world—or in her case, an absence of childhood cancer—was not proof of God's existence. God, she explained, was most apparent when beauty and light could be found in the darkest of places, for example, in a hospital filled with children fighting against (and even dying from) cancer. I didn't understand what Lisa meant for a long time, though I probably pretended I did. But as time continues to tick away, I continue to grow in my understanding of where God can be found. And for whatever reason, darkness is one of these places.

In a book I studied in my last religious studies class at Rhodes, Edward Edinger writes in the terminology of Jung that the ego must be in a humbled state of darkness and need before it can perceive the dim light of the transpersonal psyche.[1] In less confusing psychological terms, we are

1. Edinger, *The Bible and the Psyche.*